Christmas In Legend And Story

A BOOK FOR BOYS AND GIRLS

ELVA S. SMITH

[ZHINGOORA BOOKS]

This edition is published by
Zhingoora Books.

The Cover is Designed by Pallav Sethiya.

CONTENTS

CHRISTMAS IN LEGEND AND STORY

"THE GRACIOUS TIME"

According to tradition, on the Holy Night there fell upon Bethlehem of Judea a strange and unnatural calm; the voices of the birds were hushed, water ceased to flow and the wind was stilled. But when the child Jesus was born all nature burst into new life; trees put forth green leaves, grass sprang up and bright flowers bloomed. To animals was granted the power of human speech and the ox and the ass knelt in their stalls in adoration of the infant Saviour. Then it was that the shepherds abiding in the field with their flocks heard the angels praising God, and kings of the Orient watching in their "far country" saw ablaze in the heavens the long-expected sign. Even in distant Rome there sprang up a well or fountain which "ran largely" and the ancient prophetess, Sibyl, looking eastward from the Capitoline hill heard the angel song and saw in vision all the wonders of that night.

There are many such traditional tales of the nativity, of the "star-led wizards" and of the marvels wrought by the boy Christ. They tell of the bees singing their sweet hymn of praise to the Lord, of the palm-tree bending down its branches that the weary travellers fleeing from the wrath of Herod might be refreshed by its fruit, of the juniper which opened to conceal them and of the sweet-smelling balsam which grew wherever the drops of moisture fell from the brow of the Boy "as He ran about or toiled in His loving service for His Mother." Quaint fancies some of these, perhaps, and not all of them worth preserving; but oftentimes beautiful, and with a germ of truth.

From the centuries between then and now, come stories of holy men, of bishops and peasant-saints, and of brave men who preached the White Christ to the vikings of the north or on Iona's isle. As in popular belief, with each returning eve of the nativity the miracles of the first Christmas happen again, so in these tales the thorn-tree blossoms anew and wonderful roses bloom in the bleak forest.

Other stories tell how on each Christmas eve the little Christ-child comes again to earth and wanders through village or town, while lighted candles are placed in the windows to guide Him on His way.

These various legends and traditional tales, which sprang up among the people like flowers by the wayside and became a part of the life of the Middle Ages, are still of interest to us of to-day and have a distinct charm of their own. And when the childlike faith and beauty of thought of the finest of these have found expression in literary form they seem particularly suited for our reading at "the gracious time."

THE ADORATION OF THE SHEPHERDS

ST. LUKE, II, 1-16

And it came to pass in those days, that there went out a decree from Caesar Augustus, that all the world should be taxed.

And this taxing was first made when Cyrenius was governor of Syria.

And all went to be taxed, every one into his own city.

And Joseph also went up from Galilee, out of the city of Nazareth, into Judaea, unto the city of David, which is called Bethlehem; because he was of the house and lineage of David:

To be taxed with Mary his espoused wife, being great with child.

And so it was, that, while they were there, the days were accomplished that she should be delivered.

And she brought forth her firstborn son, and wrapped him in swaddling clothes, and laid him in a manger; because there was no room for them in the inn.

And there were in the same country shepherds abiding in the field, keeping watch over their flock by night.

And, lo, the angel of the Lord came upon them, and the glory of the Lord shone round about them: and they were sore afraid.

And the angel said unto them, Fear not: for, behold, I bring you good tidings of great joy, which shall be to all people.

For unto you is born this day in the city of David a Saviour, which is Christ the Lord.

And this shall be a sign unto you; Ye shall find the babe wrapped in swaddling clothes, lying in a manger.

And suddenly there was with the angel a multitude of the heavenly host praising God, and saying,

Glory to God in the highest, and on earth peace, good will toward men.

And it came to pass, as the angels were gone away from them into heaven, the shepherds said one to another, Let us now go even unto Bethlehem, and see this thing which is come to pass, which the Lord hath made known unto us.

And they came with haste, and found Mary, and Joseph, and the babe lying in a manger.

THE CHILD BORN AT BETHLEHEM

HORACE ELISHA SCUDDER

About six miles to the south of Jerusalem is the village of Bethlehem, lying along the slope and on the top of a gray hill, from the steep eastern end of which one looks over a broad plain, toward a range of high hills beyond. At any time, as one drew near the place, coming from Jerusalem, he would pass by rounded hills, and now and then cross little ravines with brooks, sometimes full of water, sometimes only beds of stone; and, if it were spring-time, he would see the hills and valleys covered with their grass, and sprinkled abundantly with a great variety of wild flowers, daisies, poppies, the Star of Bethlehem, tulips and anemones—a broad sheet of color, of scarlet, white and green. Perhaps, very long ago, there were trees also where now there are none; and on those hills, gray with the stone that peeped out through the grass, stood the mighty cedars of Lebanon, stretching out their sweeping branches, and oaks, sturdy and rich with dark foliage, green the year round. At any rate, then, as now, we may believe that there were vineyards upon the sunny slopes, and we know that the wind blew over corn-fields covering the plains that lay between the ranges of hills.

It is of the time long since that we are thinking, when there were no massive buildings on Bethlehem hill, such as are to be seen in the town as it now appears. Instead, there were low houses, many of mud and sunburnt brick, some so poor, doubtless, that the cattle were stalled, if not in the same room with the people of the house, yet so near that they could be heard through the partition, stamping, and crunching their food. There was an inn there, also; but we must not think of it as like our modern public-houses, with a landlord and servants, where one could have what he needed by paying for it. Rather, it was a collection of buildings for the convenience and accommodation of travelers, who brought with them whatever they required of food, and the means of preparing it, finding there only shelter and the roughest conveniences. The larger inns of this sort were built in the form of a great courtyard surrounded by arcades, in which people stayed, and kept their goods, if they were merchants.

The inn at Bethlehem was not probably one of these great caravanserais,—as they are called now in the East, because caravans stop at them; and it is even possible that the stables about the inn were simply caves scooped out of the soft chalk rock, for the country there has an abundance of these caves used for this very purpose.

From the hill on which Bethlehem stands, one can see travelers approaching, and at that time, long ago, no doubt the people who lived there saw companies of travelers, on foot or mounted, coming up to the village. For it was a busy time in Judea. The Emperor at Rome, the capital of the world, had ordered a tax to be laid upon his subjects, and first it had to be known just who were liable to be taxed. Nowadays, and in our country, people have their names taken down at the door of their own houses, and pay their tax in the town where they live. But then, in Judea, it was different. If a man had always lived in one place, and his parents before him, well and good: there his name was taken down, and there he was taxed. But if he was of a family that had left another place, he went back to the old home, and there his name was registered. There were many, it may be, who at this time were visiting Bethlehem for this purpose.

At least, we know of two amongst these travelers; devout and humble people they were; Joseph, a carpenter, living in Nazareth, a village of Galilee, sixty miles or more to the northward, and Mary, his wife. Together they were coming to Bethlehem, for while Nazareth was now their home, they were sprung from a family that once lived in Bethlehem, and though they were now poor and lowly, that family was the royal family, and King David, the greatest king that ever sat on the Jewish throne, was their ancestor. Perhaps, as they climbed the hill, they thought of Ruth, who had gleaned in the corn-fields just where they were passing, and no doubt they thought of Ruth's great-grandson, King David, who was born here, and here kept his father's sheep,—such sheep as even now they could see on the hillsides, watched by the watching shepherds.

They came, like the rest, to the caravanserai, but found it already filled with travelers. They could not have room with other men and women, and yet there was shelter to be had, for the place where the horses and beasts of burden stood was not all taken up. It may be that many of those now occupying the inn had come on Joseph's errand, and, not being merchants, had come unattended by the beasts that bore the goods of merchants, who were there occupying the inn; and what were they there for? We can only guess. All is forgotten of that gathering; men remember only the two travelers from Nazareth who could find no room in the inn, and made their resting-place by a manger.

For there, away from the crowd, was born to Mary a child, whom she wrapped in swaddling-clothes and laid in the manger. She was away from home; she was not even in a friend's house, nor yet in the inn; the Lord God had made ready a crib for the babe in the feeding-place of cattle. What gathering of friends could there be to rejoice over a child born in this solitary place?

Yet there were some, friends of the child and of the child's mother, who welcomed its birth with great rejoicing. It may be that when Mary was laying Him upon His first hard earthly resting-place, there was, not far off, such a sight as never before was seen on earth. On the hilly slopes about Bethlehem were flocks of sheep that, day and night, cropped the grass, watched by shepherds, just as, so long before, young David, in the same place, had watched his father's sheep. These shepherds were devout men, who sang, we may easily believe, the songs which the shepherd David had taught them; and now, in the night-time, on the quiet slopes, as they kept guard over their flocks, out of the darkness appeared a heavenly visitor: whence he came they knew not, but round about him was a brightness which they knew could be no other than the brightness of His presence which God cast about His messengers. Great fear fell upon them—for who of mortals could stand before the heavenly beings? But the angel, quick to see their fear, spoke in words which were the words of men and fell in peaceful accents:—

"Fear not!" said he, "for see, I bring you glad tidings of a great joy that shall be to all the people. For there has been born to you, this very day, a Saviour, who is the Holy Lord, born in the city of David; and this shall be its sign to you: ye shall find a child wrapped in swaddling-clothes lying in a manger."

And now, suddenly, before they could speak to the heavenly messenger, they saw, not him alone, but the place full of the like heavenly beings. A multitude was there; they came not as if from some distant place, but as angels that ever stood round these shepherds. The eyes of the men were opened, and they saw, besides the grassy slopes and feeding sheep, and distant Bethlehem, and the stars above, a host of angels. Their ears were opened, and besides the moving sheep and rustling boughs, they heard from this great army of heavenly beings a song, rising to God and falling like a blessing upon the sleeping world:—

"Glory to God in the highest
  And on earth peace,
  Good will to men."

In the lowly manger, a little child; on the hillside pasture, a heavenly host singing His praises! Then it was once more quiet, and the darkness was about the shepherds. They looked at one another and said,—"Let us go, indeed, to Bethlehem, to see this thing that has come to pass, which the Lord hath made us know."

So, in all haste, with the sound of that hymn of glory in their ears, they left the pasture and sought the town. They went to the inn, but they looked not there for the child; where the mangers were, there they sought Him, and found Him lying, and by Him Joseph and Mary. There were others by the new-born child, some who had doubtless come out from the inn at hearing of the birth. "Whence are these shepherds?" they might have said to themselves, "and what has brought them to this birthplace?"

To all by the manger, the shepherds, their minds full of the strange sight they had witnessed, recount the marvel. They tell how one appeared with such brightness about him as in old times they had heard gave witness that the Lord God would speak to His people; how their fear at his presence was quieted by his strange and joyful words; and how, when he had said, "Ye shall find a child wrapped in swaddling-clothes, lying in a manger," they suddenly were aware of a host of angels round about them sounding praise, to which God also listened.

Those to whom they told these things were amazed indeed at the strangeness. What did the marvel mean, they wondered. They could know no more than the shepherds had told them, and as for these men, they went away to their flocks again, praising God, for now they too, had seen the child, and it was all true, and with their human voice they caught up the song of rejoicing which had fallen from angelic lips.

There was one who heard it all, and we may think did not say much or ask much, but laid it away in her heart. It was Mary, and she had, in the treasure-house where she put away this wonder, other thoughts and recollections in company with it. There, in her inmost heart, she kept the remembrance of a heavenly visitor who had appeared to her when she was alone, and had quieted her fear by words that told her of this coming birth, and filled her soul with the thought that He whom she should bear was to have the long-deserted throne and a kingdom without end. She remembered how, when she visited her cousin Elizabeth, she was greeted with a psalm of rejoicing that sprang to the lips of that holy woman, and from her own heart had come a psalm of response.

And now the child was born—born in the place of David, yet born to be laid in a manger. A name had been given it by the angel, and she called the child Jesus; for Jesus means Saviour, and "He shall," said the angel, "save His people from their sins."

AS JOSEPH WAS A-WALKING

OLD ENGLISH CAROL

As Joseph was a-walking
  He heard an angel sing:—
"This night there shall be born
  Our heavenly King.

"He neither shall be born
  In housen, nor in hall,
Nor in the place of Paradise,
  But in an ox's stall.

"He neither shall be clothèd
  In purple nor in pall;
But in the fair, white linen,
  That usen babies all.

"He neither shall be rockèd
  In silver nor in gold,
But in a wooden cradle
  That rocks on the mould.

"He neither shall be christened
  In white wine nor in red,
But with fair spring water
  With which we were christened."

Mary took her baby,
  She dressed Him so sweet,
She laid Him in a manger,
  All there for to sleep.

As she stood over Him
  She heard angels sing,
"O bless our dear Saviour,
  Our heavenly King."

THE PEACEFUL NIGHT

JOHN MILTON

But peaceful was the night
Wherein the Prince of Light
  His reign of peace upon the earth began.
The winds with wonder whist,
Smoothly the waters kist,
  Whispering new joys to the mild Ocean,—
Who now hath quite forgot to rave,
While birds of calm sit brooding on the charmed wave.

The stars, with deep amaze,
Stand fixed in steadfast gaze,
  Bending one way their precious influence;
And will not take their flight,
For all the morning light,
  Or Lucifer that often warned them thence;
But in their glimmering orbs did glow,
Until their Lord himself bespake, and bid them
  go.

And, though the shady gloom
Had given day her room,
  The sun himself withheld his wonted speed,
And hid his head for shame,
As his inferior flame
  The new-enlightened world no more should need:
He saw a greater Sun appear
Than his bright throne or burning axletree could bear.

THE CHRISTMAS SILENCE

MARGARET DELAND

Hushed are the pigeons cooing low
  On dusty rafters of the loft;
  And mild-eyed oxen, breathing soft,
Sleep on the fragrant hay below.

Dim shadows in the corner hide;
  The glimmering lantern's rays are shed
  Where one young lamb just lifts his head,
Then huddles 'gainst his mother's side.

Strange silence tingles in the air;
  Through the half-open door a bar
  Of light from one low-hanging star
Touches a baby's radiant hair.

No sound: the mother, kneeling, lays
  Her cheek against the little face.
  Oh human love! Oh heavenly grace!
'Tis yet in silence that she prays!

Ages of silence end to-night;
  Then to the long-expectant earth
  Glad angels come to greet His birth
In burst of music, love, and light!

NEIGHBORS OF THE CHRIST NIGHT

NORA ARCHIBALD SMITH

Deep in the shelter of the cave,
　The ass with drooping head
Stood weary in the shadow, where
　His master's hand had led.
About the manger oxen lay,
　Bending a wide-eyed gaze
Upon the little new-born Babe,
　Half worship, half amaze.
High in the roof the doves were set,
　And cooed there, soft and mild,
Yet not so sweet as, in the hay,
　The Mother to her Child.
The gentle cows breathed fragrant breath
　To keep Babe Jesus warm,
While loud and clear, o'er hill and dale,
　The cocks crowed, "Christ is born!"
Out in the fields, beneath the stars,
　The young lambs sleeping lay,
And dreamed that in the manger slept
　Another, white as they.

These were Thy neighbors, Christmas Child;
　To Thee their love was given,
For in Thy baby face there shone
　The wonder-light of Heaven.

CHRISTMAS CAROL

FROM THE NEAPOLITAN

When Christ was born in Bethlehem,
'T was night, but seemed the noon of day;
  The stars, whose light
  Was pure and bright,
Shone with unwavering ray;
But one, one glorious star
Guided the Eastern Magi from afar.

Then peace was spread throughout the land;
The lion fed beside the tender lamb;
  And with the kid,
  To pasture led,
  The spotted leopard fed;
In peace, the calf and bear,
The wolf and lamb reposed together there.

As shepherds watched their flocks by night,
An angel, brighter than the sun's own light,
    Appeared in air,
    And gently said,
    Fear not,—be not afraid,
For lo! beneath your eyes,
Earth has become a smiling paradise.

A CHRISTMAS HYMN

RICHARD WATSON GILDER

Tell me what is this innumerable throng
Singing in the heavens a loud angelic song?
These are they who come with swift and shining feet
From round about the throne of God the Lord of Light to greet.

Oh, who are these that hasten beneath the starry sky,
As if with joyful tidings that through the world shall fly?
The faithful shepherds these, who greatly were afeared
When, as they watched their flocks by night, the heavenly host appeared.

Who are these that follow across the hills of night
A star that westward hurries along the fields of light?

Three wise men from the east who myrrh and treasure bring
To lay them at the feet of him their Lord and Christ and King.

What babe new-born is this that in a manger cries?
Near on her lowly bed his happy mother lies.
Oh, see the air is shaken with white and heavenly wings—
This is the Lord of all the earth, this is the King of kings.

THE SONG OF A SHEPHERD—BOY AT BETHLEHEM

JOSEPHINE PRESTON PEABODY

Sleep, Thou little Child of Mary:
   Rest Thee now.
Though these hands be rough from shearing
   And the plough,

Yet they shall not ever fail Thee,
When the waiting nations hail Thee,
Bringing palms unto their King.
   Now—I sing.

Sleep, Thou little Child of Mary,
   Hope divine.
If Thou wilt but smile upon me,
   I will twine
Blossoms for Thy garlanding.
Thou'rt so little to be King,
   God's Desire!
   Not a brier
Shall be left to grieve Thy brow;
   Rest Thee now.

Sleep, Thou little Child of Mary.
  Some fair day
Wilt Thou, as Thou wert a brother,
  Come away
Over hills and over hollow?
All the lambs will up and follow,
Follow but for love of Thee.
  Lov'st Thou me?

23

Sleep, Thou little Child of Mary;
  Rest Thee now.
I that watch am come from sheep-stead
  And from plough.
Thou wilt have disdain of me
When Thou'rt lifted, royally,
Very high for all to see:
  Smilest Thou?

THE FIRST CHRISTMAS ROSES

ADAPTED FROM AN OLD LEGEND

The sun had dropped below the western hills of Judea, and the stillness of night had covered the earth. The heavens were illumined only by numberless stars, which shone the brighter for the darkness of the sky. No sound was heard but the occasional howl of a jackal or the bleat of a lamb in the sheepfold. Inside a tent on the hillside slept the shepherd, Berachah, and his daughter, Madelon. The little girl lay restless,— sleeping, waking, dreaming, until at last she roused herself and looked about her.

"Father," she whispered, "oh, my father, awake. I fear for the sheep."

The shepherd turned himself and reached for his staff. "What nearest thou, daughter! The dogs are asleep. Hast thou been burdened by an evil dream?"

"Nay, but father," she answered, "seest thou not the light? Hearest thou not the voice?"

Berachah gathered his mantle about him, rose, looked over the hills toward Bethlehem, and listened. The olive trees on yonder slope were casting their shadows in a marvellous light, unlike daybreak or sunset, or even the light of the moon. By the camp-fire below on the hillside the shepherds on watch were rousing themselves. Berachah waited and wondered, while Madelon clung to his side. Suddenly a sound rang out in the stillness. Madelon pressed still closer.

"It is the voice of an angel, my daughter. What it means I know not. Neither understand I this light." Berachah fell on his knees and prayed.

"Fear not: for, behold, I bring you good tidings of great joy, which shall be to all people. For unto you is born this day in the city of David a Saviour, which is Christ the Lord. And this shall be a sign unto you; Ye shall find the babe wrapped in swaddling clothes, lying in a manger."

The voice of the angel died away, and the air was filled with music. Berachah raised Madelon to her feet. "Ah, daughter," said he, "It is the wonder night so long expected. To us hath it been given to see the sign. It is the Messiah who hath come, the Messiah, whose name shall be called Wonderful, Counsellor, the mighty God, the Everlasting Father, the Prince of Peace. He it is who shall reign on the throne of David, he it is who shall redeem Israel."

Slowly up the hillside toiled the shepherds to the tent of Berachah, their chief, who rose to greet them eagerly.

"What think you of the wonder night and of the sign?" he queried. "Are we not above all others honored, thus to learn of the Messiah's coming!"

"Yea, and Berachah," replied their spokesman, Simon, "believest thou not that we should worship the infant King! Let us now go to Bethlehem, and see this thing which has come to pass."

A murmur of protest came from the edge of the circle, and one or two turned impatiently away, whispering of duty toward flocks, and the folly of searching for a new-born baby in the city of Bethlehem. Hardheaded, practical men were these, whose hearts had not been touched by vision or by song.

The others, however, turned expectantly toward Berachah, awaiting his decision. "Truly," said Jude, "the angel of the Lord hath given us the sign in order that we might go to worship Him. How can we then do otherwise? We shall find Him, as we have heard, lying in a manger. Let us not tarry, but let us gather our choicest treasures to lay at His feet, and set out without delay across the hills toward Bethlehem."

"Oh, my father," whispered Madelon, "permit me to go with thee." Berachah did not hear her, but turned and bade the men gather together their gifts.

"I, too, father?" asked Madelon. Still Berachah said nothing. Madelon slipped back into the tent, and throwing her arms around Melampo, her shepherd dog, whispered in his ear.

Soon the shepherds returned with their gifts. Simple treasures they were,—a pair of doves, a fine wool blanket, some eggs, some honey, some late autumn fruits. Berachah had searched for the finest of his flock,—a snow-white lamb. Across the hills toward Bethlehem in the quiet, star-lit night they journeyed. As they moved silently along, the snow beneath their feet was changed to grass and flowers, and the icicles which had dropped from the trees covered their pathway like stars in the Milky Way.

Following at a distance, yet close enough to see them, came Madelon with Melampo at her heels. Over the hills they travelled on until Madelon lost sight of their own hillside. Farther and farther the shepherds went until they passed David's well, and entered the city. Berachah led the way.

"How shall we know?" whispered Simon. And the others answered, "Hush, we must await the sign."

When at last they had compassed the crescent of Bethlehem's hills, they halted by an open doorway at a signal from their leader. "The manger," they joyfully murmured, "the manger! We have found the new-born King!"

One by one the shepherds entered. One by one they fell on their knees. Away in the shadow stood the little girl, her hand on Melampo's head. In wonder she gazed while the shepherds presented their gifts, and were permitted each to hold for a moment the newborn Saviour.

Melampo, the shepherd dog, crouched on the ground, as if he too, like the ox and the ass within, would worship the Child. Madelon turned toward the darkness weeping. Then, lifting her face to heaven, she prayed that God would bless Mother and Baby. Melampo moved closer to her, dumbly offering his companionship, and, raising his head, seemed to join in her petition. Once more she looked at the worshipping circle.

"Alas," she grieved, "no gift have I for the infant Saviour. Would that I had but a flower to place in His hand."

Suddenly Melampo stirred by her side, and as she turned again from the manger she saw before her an angel, the light from whose face illumined the darkness, and whose look of tenderness rested on her tear-stained eyes.

"Why grievest thou, maiden?" asked the angel.

"That I come empty-handed to the cradle of the Saviour, that I bring no gift to greet Him," she murmured.

"The gift of thine heart, that is the best of all," answered the angel. "But that thou mayst carry something to the manger, see, I will strike with my staff upon the ground."

Wonderingly Madelon waited. From the dry earth wherever the angel's staff had touched sprang fair, white roses. Timidly she stretched out her hand toward the nearest ones. In the light of the angel's smile she gathered them, until her arms were filled with flowers. Again she turned toward the manger, and quietly slipped to the circle of kneeling shepherds.

Closer she crept to the Child, longing, yet fearing, to offer her gift.

"How shall I know," she pondered, "whether He will receive this my gift as His own?"

Berachah gazed in amazement at Madelon and the roses which she held. How came his child there, his child whom he had left safe on the hillside? And whence came such flowers! Truly this was a wonder night.

Step by step she neared the manger, knelt, and placed a rose in the Baby's hand. As the shepherds watched in silence, Mary bent over her Child, and Madelon waited for a sign. "Will He accept them?" she questioned. "How, oh, how shall I know?" As she prayed in humble silence, the Baby's eyes opened slowly, and over His face spread a smile.

THE LITTLE GRAY LAMB

ARCHIBALD BERESFORD SULLIVAN

Out on the endless purple hills, deep in the clasp of somber night, The
shepherds guarded their weary ones— guarded their flocks of cloudy
white, That like a snowdrift in silence lay, Save one little lamb with its
fleece of gray.

Out on the hillside all alone, gazing afar with
  sleepless eyes,
The little gray lamb prayed soft and low, its
  weary face to the starry skies:
"O moon of the heavens so fair, so bright,
Give me—oh, give me—a fleece of white!"

No answer came from the dome of blue, nor comfort lurked in the
cypress-trees; But faint came a whisper borne along on the scented wings
of the passing breeze: "Little gray lamb that prays this night, I cannot
give thee a fleece of white."

Then the little gray lamb of the sleepless eyes
  prayed to the clouds for a coat of snow,
Asked of the roses, besought the woods; but
  each gave answer sad and low:
  "Little gray lamb that prays this night,
  We cannot give thee a fleece of white."

Like a gem unlocked from a casket dark, like
  an ocean pearl from its bed of blue,
Came, softly stealing the clouds between, a
  wonderful star which brighter grew
  Until it flamed like the sun by day
  Over the place where Jesus lay.

Ere hushed were the angels' notes of praise
   the joyful shepherds had quickly sped
Past rock and shadow, adown the hill, to kneel
   at the Saviour's lowly bed;
  While, like the spirits of phantom night,
  Followed their flocks—their flocks of white.

And patiently, longingly, out of the night,
   apart from the others,—far apart,—
Came limping and sorrowful, all alone, the
   little gray lamb of the weary heart,
  Murmuring, "I must bide far away:
  I am not worthy—my fleece is gray."

And the Christ Child looked upon humbled
   pride, at kings bent low on the earthen floor,
But gazed beyond at the saddened heart of the
   little gray lamb at the open door;
And he called it up to his manger low and laid
   his hand on its wrinkled face,
While the kings drew golden robes aside to
   give to the weary one a place.
  And the fleece of the little gray lamb was blest:
  For, lo! it was whiter than all the rest!

* * * * *

In many cathedrals grand and dim, whose windows
   glimmer with pane and lens,
Mid the odor of incense raised in prayer, hallowed
   about with last amens,
The infant Saviour is pictured fair, with
   kneeling Magi wise and old,

But his baby-hand rests—not on the gifts, the
  myrrh, the frankincense, the gold—
  But on the head, with a heavenly light,
  Of the little gray lamb that was changed to white.

THE HOLY NIGHT

ELIZABETH BARRETT BROWNING

We sate among the stalls at Bethlehem;
The dumb kine from their fodder turning them,
  Softened their horned faces
  To almost human gazes
  Toward the newly Born:
The simple shepherds from the star-lit brooks
  Brought visionary looks,
As yet in their astonied hearing rung
  The strange sweet angel-tongue:
The magi of the East, in sandals worn,
  Knelt reverent, sweeping round,
  With long pale beards, their gifts upon the ground,
  The incense, myrrh, and gold
These baby hands were impotent to hold:
So let all earthlies and celestials wait
  Upon thy royal state.
  Sleep, sleep, my kingly One!

THE STAR BEARER

EDMUND CLARENCE STEDMAN

There were seven angels erst that spanned
  Heaven's roadway out through space,
Lighting with stars, by God's command,
  The fringe of that high place
Whence plumèd beings in their joy,
The servitors His thoughts employ,
  Fly ceaselessly. No goodlier band
    Looked upward to His face.

There, on bright hovering wings that tire
  Never, they rested mute,
Nor of far journeys had desire,
  Nor of the deathless fruit;
For in and through each angel soul
All waves of life and knowledge roll,
  Even as to nadir streamed the fire
    Of their torches resolute.

They lighted Michael's outpost through
  Where fly the armored brood,
And the wintry Earth their omens knew
  Of Spring's beatitude;
Rude folk, ere yet the promise came,
Gave to their orbs a heathen name,
  Saying how steadfast in men's view
    The watchful Pleiads stood.

All in the solstice of the year,
  When the sun apace must turn,

The seven bright angels 'gan to hear
  Heaven's twin gates outward yearn:
Forth with its light and minstrelsy
A lordly troop came speeding by,
  And joyed to see each cresset sphere
    So gloriously burn.

Staying his fearless passage then
  The Captain of that host
Spake with strong voice: "We bear to men
  God's gift the uttermost,
Whereof the oracle and sign
Sibyl and sages may divine:
  A star shall blazon in their ken,
    Borne with us from your post.

"This night the Heir of Heaven's throne
  A new-born mortal lies!
Since Earth's first morning hath not shone
  Such joy in seraph eyes."
He spake. The least in honor there
Answered with longing like a prayer,—
  "My star, albeit thenceforth unknown,
    Shall light for you Earth's skies."

Onward the blessed legion swept,
  That angel at the head;
(Where seven of old their station kept
  There are six that shine instead.)
Straight hitherward came troop and star;
Like some celestial bird afar
  Into Earth's night the cohort leapt
    With beauteous wings outspread.

Dazzling the East beneath it there,
  The Star gave out its rays:
Right through the still Judean air
  The shepherds see it blaze,—
They see the plume-borne heavenly throng,
And hear a burst of that high song
  Of which in Paradise aware
    Saints count their years but days.

For they sang such music as, I deem,
  In God's chief court of joys,
Had stayed the flow of the crystal stream
  And made souls in mid-flight poise;
They sang of Glory to Him most High,
Of Peace on Earth abidingly,
  And of all delights the which, men dream,
    Nor sin nor grief alloys.

Breathless the kneeling shepherds heard,
  Charmed from their first rude fear,
Nor while that music dwelt had stirred
  Were it a month or year:
And Mary Mother drank its flow,
Couched with her Babe divine,—and, lo!
  Ere falls the last ecstatic word
    Three Holy Kings draw near.

Whenas the star-led shining train
  Wheeled from their task complete,
Skyward from over Bethlehem's plain
  They sped with rapture fleet;
And the angel of that orient star,
Thenceforth where Heaven's lordliest are,

Stands with a harp, while Christ doth reign,
  A seraph near His feet.

THE VISIT OF THE WISE MEN

ST. MATTHEW, II, 1-12

Now when Jesus was born in Bethlehem of Judaea in the days of Herod the king, behold, there came wise men from the east to Jerusalem,

Saying, Where is he that is born King of the Jews? for we have seen his star in the east, and are come to worship him.

When Herod the king had heard these things, he was troubled, and all Jerusalem with him.

And when he had gathered all the chief priests and scribes of the people together, he demanded of them where Christ should be born.

And they said unto him, In Bethlehem of Judaea: for thus it is written by the prophet,

And thou Bethlehem, in the land of Judah, art not the least among the princes of Judah: for out of thee shall come a Governor, that shall rule my people Israel.

Then Herod, when he had privily called the wise men, inquired of them diligently what time the star appeared.

And he sent them to Bethlehem, and said, Go and search diligently for the young child; and when ye have found him, bring me word again, that I may come and worship him also.

When they had heard the king, they departed; and, lo, the star, which they saw in the east, went before them, till it came and stood over where the young child was.

When they saw the star, they rejoiced with exceeding great joy.

And when they were come into the house, they saw the young child with Mary his mother, and fell down, and worshipped him: and when they had opened their treasures, they presented unto him gifts; gold, and frankincense, and myrrh.

And being warned of God in a dream that they should not return to Herod, they departed into their own country another way.

THE THREE KINGS

HENRY WADSWORTH LONGFELLOW

Three Kings came riding from far away,
Melchior and Gaspar and Baltasar;
Three Wise Men out of the East were they,
And they travelled by night and they slept by day,
For their guide was a beautiful, wonderful star.

The star was so beautiful, large, and clear,
  That all the other stars of the sky
Became a white mist in the atmosphere,
And by this they knew that the coming was near
  Of the Prince foretold in the prophecy.

Three caskets they bore on their saddle-bows,
  Three caskets of gold with golden keys;
Their robes were of crimson silk with rows
Of bells and pomegranates and furbelows,
  Their turbans like blossoming almond-trees.

And so the Three Kings rode into the West,
  Through the dusk of night, over hill and dell,
And sometimes they nodded with beard on breast,
And sometimes talked, as they paused to rest,
  With the people they met at some wayside well.

"Of the child that is born," said Baltasar,
  "Good people, I pray you, tell us the news;
For we in the East have seen his star,
And have ridden fast, and have ridden far,
  To find and worship the King of the Jews."

And the people answered, "You ask in vain;
  We know of no king but Herod the Great!"
They thought the Wise Men were men insane,
As they spurred their horses across the plain,
  Like riders in haste, and who cannot wait.

And when they came to Jerusalem,
  Herod the Great, who had heard this thing,
Sent for the Wise Men and questioned them;
And said, "Go down unto Bethlehem,
  And bring me tidings of this new king."

So they rode away; and the star stood still,
  The only one in the gray of morn;
Yes, it stopped,—it stood still of its own free will,
Right over Bethlehem on the hill,
  The city of David, where Christ was born.

And the Three Kings rode through the gate and the guard,
  Through the silent street, till their horses turned
And neighed as they entered the great inn-yard;
But the windows were closed, and the doors were barred,
  And only a light in the stable burned.

And cradled there in the scented hay,
  In the air made sweet by the breath of kine,
The little child in the manger lay,
The child, that would be king one day
  Of a kingdom not human but divine.

His mother Mary of Nazareth
  Sat watching beside his place of rest,
Watching the even flow of his breath,

For the joy of life and the terror of death
  Were mingled together in her breast.

They laid their offerings at his feet:
  The gold was their tribute to a King,
The frankincense, with its odor sweet,
Was for the Priest, the Paraclete,
  The myrrh for the body's burying.

And the mother wondered and bowed her head,
  And sat as still as a statue of stone;
Her heart was troubled yet comforted,
Remembering what the Angel had said
  Of an endless reign and of David's throne.

Then the Kings rode out of the city gate,
  With a clatter of hoofs in proud array;
But they went not back to Herod the Great,
For they knew his malice and feared his hate,
  And returned to their homes by another way.

THE THREE HOLY KINGS

ADAPTED FROM THE GOLDEN LEGEND, AND OTHER SOURCES

In a far country, in the days before Jesus was born in Judea, there were great astrologers who studied the heavens by night and by day, for they knew of the prophecy which said that a star shall be born or spring out of Jacob, and a man shall arise of the lineage of Israel. And twelve of them were chosen to take heed, who every year ascended upon a mountain which was called the Hill of Victory. Three days they abode there, and prayed our Lord that He would show to them the star that Balaam had said and prophesied.

Now it happened on a time, that they were there on the day of the Nativity of Jesus Christ, and a star came over them upon this mountain, which had the form of a right fair child, and under his head was a shining cross, and from this cross came a voice saying: "To-day is there born a King in Judea."

Now in Arabia, the land in which the soil is red with gold, there reigned a king called Melchior. And in Saba, where frankincense flows from the trees, the king Balthasar ruled. And in the land where myrrh hangs from the bushes, the kingdom of Tharsis, reigned a third king, called Caspar. These three kings also saw the star and heard the voice, and they each made ready to go on a journey. And no one of the three knew that the others intended thus to make a pilgrimage. And they gathered together their treasures to present to the king whom they should seek, and summoned those who should attend them. So each set out with a great company and great estate. And as they journeyed they found the mountains made level as the plains, while the swollen rivers became as dry land. And never did they lose sight of the star, which shined upon them as the sun, always moving before them to guide them on their way.

But when they were come within two miles of Jerusalem, the star disappeared, a heavy fog arose, and each party halted; Melchior, as it fell out, taking his stand on Mount Calvary, Balthasar on the Mount of Olives, and Caspar just between them. And when the fog cleared away, each was astonished to see two other great companies besides his own, and then the kings first discovered that all had come upon the same errand, and they embraced with great joy, and rode together into Jerusalem.

And when they came into the city, Herod and all the people were troubled, because of their so great company like unto an army. Then they demanded in what place the King of the Jews was born, for, said they, "We have seen His star in the Orient, and therefore we come to worship Him." And when Herod had heard this, he was much troubled, and all Jerusalem with him. Then Herod called all the priests of the law, and the doctors, and demanded of them where Jesus Christ should be born. And when he had understood them that He should be born in Bethlehem, he called the three kings apart and demanded of them diligently the time that the star appeared to them. And he said to them that as soon as they should have found the Child and have worshipped Him, that they should return and show it to him, feigning that he would worship Him also, though he thought that he would go to slay Him.

And as soon as the kings were entered into Jerusalem, the sight of the star was taken from them. But when they were issued out of the city, the star appeared again and went before them, until it came above the place in Bethlehem where the Child was. And they had journeyed now full thirteen days.

And when they had entered into the place they worshipped the young Child, and Mary, His mother. Now the kings had brought great treasures with them, for it must be known that all that Alexander the Great left at his death, and all that the Queen of Sheba gave to King Solomon, and all that Solomon collected for the temple, had descended to the three kings from their ancestors; and all this they had now brought with them. But when they had bowed down before the Child, they were filled with fear and amazement because of the so great light which was in the place. And they each offered quickly the first thing that came to their hands, and forgot all their other gifts. Melchior offered thirty golden pennies, Balthasar gave frankincense, and Caspar myrrh; but all else they quite forgot, and only remembered that they bowed before the Child, and said "Thanks be to God."

And when they would have stayed to do honor to the Holy Child, an angel came to them in a dream, to warn them against Herod, who would do them harm. So they departed each to his own country, journeying for two years. And they preached unto the people, telling them of the new-born King, and everywhere upon the temples men placed the figures of a star, the Child, and a cross.

Now it happened years later that St. Thomas the Apostle journeyed to the far country to preach, and that he wondered why the star was placed upon the temples. Then the priests in those temples told him about the three kings and how they had journeyed to Bethlehem and had seen the young Child.

And the three kings were very old and feeble, but when they heard about St. Thomas, each set out from his own place to go to meet him. And when they had come together they builded them a city, and lived together there for two years, worshipping God and preaching. Then Melchior died, and was buried in a large and costly tomb. And when Balthasar died, he, too, was buried there. And at last Caspar was placed beside his companions.

Now in the days of Constantine the Great, his mother Helena determined to find the bodies of the three kings, and for this she made a journey to the far country. And when she had found them, she brought them to Constantinople to the Church of St. Sophia, where they were held in much honor. And from Constantinople they were taken to Milan, where again many pilgrims came. Now when Frederick Barbarossa laid siege to the city of Milan, he rejoiced above all else to find them there. And by him they were taken to Cologne, and there a golden shrine was built in which the bones of the three holy kings were placed that there they might remain until the Judgment day.

THE THREE KINGS OF COLOGNE

EUGENE FIELD

From out Cologne there came three kings
  To worship Jesus Christ, their King.
To Him they sought fine herbs they brought,
  And many a beauteous golden thing;
  They brought their gifts to Bethlehem town,
  And in that manger set them down.

Then spake the first king, and he said:
  "O Child, most heavenly, bright, and fair!
I bring this crown to Bethlehem town.
  For Thee, and only Thee, to wear;
  So give a heavenly crown to me
  When I shall come at last to Thee!"

The second, then. "I bring Thee here
  This royal robe, O Child!" he cried;
"Of silk 'tis spun, and such an one
  There is not in the world beside;
So in the day of doom requite
Me with a heavenly robe of white!"

The third king gave his gift, and quoth:
  "Spikenard and myrrh to Thee I bring,
And with these twain would I most fain
  Anoint the body of my King;
  So may their incense sometime rise
  To plead for me in yonder skies!"

Thus spake the three kings of Cologne,
  That gave their gifts and went their way;

And now kneel I in prayer hard by
  The cradle of the Child to-day;
  Nor crown, nor robe, nor spice I bring
  As offering unto Christ, my King.

Yet have I brought a gift the Child
  May not despise, however small;
For here I lay my heart to-day,
  And it is full of love to all.
  Take Thou the poor but loyal thing,
  My only tribute, Christ, my King!

BABOUSCKA

ADELAIDE SKEEL

If you were a Russian child you would not watch to see Santa Klaus come down the chimney; but you would stand by the windows to catch a peep at poor Babouscka as she hurries by.

Who is Babouscka? Is she Santa Klaus' wife?

No, indeed. She is only a poor little crooked wrinkled old woman, who comes at Christmas time into everybody's house, who peeps into every cradle, turns back every coverlid, drops a tear on the baby's white pillow, and goes away very sorrowful.

And not only at Christmas time, but through all the cold winter, and especially in March, when the wind blows loud, and whistles and howls and dies away like a sigh, the Russian children hear the rustling step of the Babouscka. She is always in a hurry. One hears her running fast along the crowded streets and over the quiet country fields. She seems to be out of breath and tired, yet she hurries on.

Whom is she trying to overtake?

She scarcely looks at the little children as they press their rosy faces against the window pane and whisper to each other, "Is the Babouscka looking for us?"

No, she will not stop; only on Christmas eve will she come up-stairs into the nursery and give each little one a present. You must not think she leaves handsome gifts such as Santa Klaus brings for you. She does not bring bicycles to the boys or French dolls to the girls. She does not come in a gay little sleigh drawn by reindeer, but hobbling along on foot, and she leans on a crutch. She has her old apron filled with candy and cheap toys, and the children all love her dearly. They watch to see her come, and when one hears a rustling, he cries, "Lo! the Babouscka!" then all others look, but one must turn one's head very quickly or she vanishes. I never saw her myself.

Best of all, she loves little babies, and often, when the tired mothers sleep, she bends over their cradles, puts her brown, wrinkled face close down to the pillow and looks very sharply.

What is she looking for?

Ah, that you can't guess unless you know her sad story.

Long, long ago, a great many yesterdays ago, the Babouscka, who was even then an old woman, was busy sweeping her little hut. She lived in the coldest corner of cold Russia, and she lived alone in a lonely place where four wide roads met. These roads were at this time white with snow, for it was winter time. In the summer, when the fields were full of flowers and the air full of sunshine and singing birds, Babouscka's home did not seem so very quiet; but in the winter, with only the snow-flakes and the shy snow-birds and the loud wind for company, the little old woman felt very cheerless. But she was a busy old woman, and as it was already twilight, and her home but half swept, she felt in a great hurry to finish her work before bed-time. You must know the Babouscka was poor and could not afford to do her work by candle-light. Presently, down the widest and the lonesomest of the white roads, there appeared a long train of people coming. They were walking slowly, and seemed to be asking each other questions as to which way they should take. As the procession came nearer, and finally stopped outside the little hut, Babouscka was frightened at the splendor. There were Three Kings, with crowns on their heads, and the jewels on the Kings' breastplates sparkled like sunlight. Their heavy fur cloaks were white with the falling snow-flakes, and the queer humpy camels on which they rode looked white as milk in the snow-storm. The harness on the camels was decorated with gold, and plates of silver adorned the saddles. The saddlecloths were of the richest Eastern stuffs, and all the servants had the dark eyes and hair of an Eastern people.

The slaves carried heavy loads on their backs, and each of the Three Kings carried a present. One carried a beautiful transparent jar, and in the fading light Babouscka could see in it a golden liquid which she knew from its color must be myrrh. Another had in his hand a richly woven bag, and it seemed to be heavy, as indeed it was, for it was full of gold. The third had a stone vase in his hand, and from the rich perfume which filled the snowy air, one could guess the vase to have been filled with incense.

Babouscka was terribly frightened, so she hid herself in her hut, and let the servants knock a long time at her door before she dared open it and answer their questions as to the road they should take to a far-away town. You know she had never studied a geography lesson in her life, was old and stupid and scared. She knew the way across the fields to the nearest village, but she knew nothing else of all the wide world full of cities. The servants scolded, but the Three Kings spoke kindly to her, and asked her to accompany them on their journey that she might show them the way as far as she knew it. They told her, in words so simple that she could not fail to understand, that they had seen a Star in the sky and were following it to a little town where a young Child lay. The snow was in the sky now, and the Star was lost out of sight.

"Who is the Child?" asked the old woman.

"He is a King, and we go to worship him," they answered. "These presents of gold, frankincense and myrrh are for Him. When we find Him we will take the crowns off our heads and lay them at His feet. Come with us, Babouscka!"

What do you suppose? Shouldn't you have thought the poor little woman would have been glad to leave her desolate home on the plains to accompany these Kings on their journey?

But the foolish woman shook her head. No, the night was dark and cheerless, and her little home was warm and cosy. She looked up into the sky, and the Star was nowhere to be seen. Besides, she wanted to put her hut in order—perhaps she would be ready to go to-morrow. But the Three Kings could not wait; so when to-morrow's sun rose they were far ahead on their journey. It seemed like a dream to poor Babouscka, for even the tracks of the camels' feet were covered by the deep white snow. Everything was the same as usual; and to make sure that the night's visitors had not been a fancy, she found her old broom hanging on a peg behind the door, where she had put it when the servants knocked.

Now that the sun was shining, and she remembered the glitter of the gold and the smell of the sweet gums and myrrh, she wished she had gone with the travellers.

And she thought a great deal about the little Baby the Three Kings had gone to worship. She had no children of her own—nobody loved her—ah, if she had only gone! The more she brooded on the thought, the more miserable she grew, till the very sight of her home became hateful to her.

It is a dreadful feeling to realize that one has lost a chance of happiness. There is a feeling called remorse that can gnaw like a sharp little tooth. Babouscka felt this little tooth cut into her heart every time she remembered the visit of the Three Kings.

After a while the thought of the Little Child became her first thought at waking and her last at night. One day she shut the door of her house forever, and set out on a long journey. She had no hope of overtaking the Three Kings, but she longed to find the Child, that she too might love and worship Him. She asked every one she met, and some people thought her crazy, but others gave her kind answers. Have you perhaps guessed that the young Child whom the Three Kings sought was our Lord himself?

People told Babouscka how He was born in a manger, and many other things which you children have learned long ago. These answers puzzled the old dame mightily. She had but one idea in her ignorant head. The Three Kings had gone to seek a Baby. She would, if not too late, seek Him too.

She forgot, I am sure, how many long years had gone by. She looked in vain for the Christ-child in His manger-cradle. She spent all her little savings in toys and candy so as to make friends with little children, that they might not run away when she came hobbling into their nurseries.

Now you know for whom she is sadly seeking when she pushes back the bed-curtains and bends down over each baby's pillow. Sometimes, when the old grandmother sits nodding by the fire, and the bigger children sleep in their beds, old Babouscka comes hobbling into the room, and whispers softly, "Is the young Child here?"

Ah, no; she has come too late, too late. But the little children know her and love her. Two thousand years ago she lost the chance of finding Him. Crooked, wrinkled, old, sick and sorry, she yet lives on, looking into each baby's face—always disappointed, always seeking. Will she find Him at last?

THE FLIGHT INTO EGYPT

SELMA LAGERLÖF

Far away, in a desert in the East, there grew, many years ago, a palm that was very, very old, and very, very tall. No one passing through the desert could help stopping to look at it, for it was much higher than other palms, and people said of it that it would surely grow to be higher than the Obelisks and Pyramids.

This great palm, standing in its loneliness, and looking over the desert, one day saw something which caused its huge crown of leaves to wave to and fro with surprise on its slender stem. On the outskirts of the desert two lonely persons were wandering. They were still so far away that even a camel would have looked no larger than an ant at that distance, but they were assuredly human beings, two who were strangers to the desert—for the palm knew the people of the desert—a man and a woman, who had neither guide, nor beasts of burden, nor tent, nor water-bag.

"Verily," said the palm to itself, "these two have come hither to die."

The palm looked quickly around.

"I am surprised," it said, "that the lions have not already gone out to seize their prey. But I do not see a single one about. Nor do I see any of the robbers of the desert. But they are sure to come.

"There awaits them a sevenfold death," thought the palm. "The lions will devour them, the serpents will sting them, thirst will consume them, the sand-storm will bury them, the robbers will kill them, the burning sun will overcome them, fear will destroy them."

The palm tried to think of something else; the fate of these two made it sad. But in the immeasurable desert around it there was not a single thing that the palm had not known and gazed at for thousands of years. Nothing could attract its attention. It was again obliged to think of the two wanderers.

"By the drought and the wind!" said the palm, invoking the two greatest enemies of life, "what is the woman carrying on her arm? I believe these mad people have a little child with them!"

The palm, which was long-sighted, as the aged generally are, saw aright. The woman carried in her arms a child, that had laid its head on her breast and was sleeping.

"The child has not even enough clothes on," said the palm. "I see that the mother has lifted up her skirt and thrown it over it. She has taken it out of its bed in great haste and hurried away with it. Now I understand: these people are fugitives.

"But they are mad, all the same," continued the palm. "If they have not an angel to protect them, they should rather have let their enemies do their worst than have taken refuge in the desert. I can imagine how it has all happened. The man is at work, the child sleeps in its cradle, the woman has gone to fetch water. When she has gone a few steps from the door she sees the enemy approaching. She rushes in, seizes the child, calls to the husband that he shall follow her, and runs away. Since then they have continued their flight the whole day; they have assuredly not rested a single moment. Yes, so it has all happened; but I say all the same, if no angel protects them—

"They are in such fear that they do not feel either fatigue or other sufferings, but I read thirst in their eyes. I think I should know the face of a thirsty man."

And when the palm began to think about thirst a fit of trembling went through its high stem, and the innumerable fronds of its long leaves curled up as if held over a fire.

"If I were a man," it said, "I would never venture into the desert. He is truly brave who ventures here without having roots reaching down to the inexhaustible water-veins. There can be danger even for palms, even for such a palm as I. Could I advise them, I would beg them to return. Their enemies could never be as cruel to them as the desert. They think perhaps that it is easy to live in the desert. But I know that even I at times have had difficulty in keeping alive. I remember once in my youth when a whirlwind threw a whole mountain of sand over me I was nearly choking. If I *could* die I should have died then."

The palm continued to think aloud, as lonely old people do.

"I hear a wonderful melodious murmur passing through my crown," it said; "all the fronds of my leaves must be moving. I do not know why the sight of these poor strangers moves me so. But this sorrowful woman is so beautiful! It reminds me of the most wonderful thing that ever happened to me."

And whilst its leaves continued their melodious rustle the palm remembered how once, long, long ago, a glorious human being had visited the oasis. It was the Queen of Sheba, accompanied by the wise King Solomon. The beautiful Queen was on her way back to her own country; the King had accompanied her part of the way, and now they were about to part. "In memory of this moment," said the Queen, "I now plant a date-kernel in the earth; and I ordain that from it shall grow a palm which shall live and grow until a King is born in Judaea greater than Solomon." And as she said this she placed the kernel in the ground, and her tears watered it.

"How can it be that I should just happen to think of this to-day?" said the palm. "Can it be possible that this woman is so beautiful that she reminds me of the most beautiful of all queens, of her at whose bidding I have lived and grown to this very day? I hear my leaves rustling stronger and stronger," said the palm, "and it sounds sorrowful, like a death-song. It is as if they prophesied that someone should soon pass away. It is well to know that it is not meant for me, inasmuch that I cannot die."

The palm thought that the death-song in its leaves must be for the two lonely wanderers. They themselves surely thought that their last hour was drawing near. One could read it in their faces when they walked past one of the skeletons of the camels that lay by the roadside. One saw it from the glances with which they watched a couple of vultures flying past. It could not be otherwise—they must perish.

They had now discovered the palm in the oasis, and hastened thither to find water. But when they at last reached it they sank down in despair, for the well was dried up. The woman, exhausted, laid down the child, and sat down crying by the side of the well. The man threw himself down by her side; he lay and beat the ground with his clenched hands. The palm heard them say to each other that they must die. It also understood from their conversation that King Herod had caused all children of two or three years of age to be killed from fear that the great expected King in Judaea had been born.

"It rustles stronger and stronger in my leaves," said the palm. "These poor fugitives have soon come to their last moment."

It also heard that they were afraid of the desert. The man said it would have been better to remain and fight the soldiers than to flee. He said that it would have been an easier death.

"God will surely help us," said the woman.

"We are all alone amongst serpents and beasts of prey," said the man. "We have no food and no water. How can God help us?"

He tore his clothes in despair and pressed his face against the earth. He was hopeless, like a man with a mortal wound in his heart.

The woman sat upright, with her hands folded upon her knees. But the glances she cast over the desert spoke of unutterable despair.

The palm heard the sorrowful rustling in its leaves grow still stronger. The woman had evidently heard it too, for she looked up to the crown of the tree, and in the same moment she involuntarily raised her arms.

"Dates, dates!" she cried.

There was such a longing in her voice, that the old palm wished it had not been any higher than the gorse, and that its dates had been as easy to reach as the red berries of the hawthorn. It knew that its crown was full of clusters of dates, but how could man reach to such a dazzling height?

The man had already seen that, the dates being so high, it was impossible to reach them. He did not even lift his head. He told his wife that she must not wish for the impossible.

But the child, which had crawled about alone and was playing with sticks and straws, heard the mother's exclamation. The little one could probably not understand why his mother should not have everything she wished for. As soon as he heard the word "dates," he began to look at the tree. He wondered and pondered how he should get the dates. There came almost wrinkles on his forehead under the fair locks. At last a smile passed over his face. Now he knew what he would do. He went to the palm, stroked it with his little hand, and said in his gentle, childish voice:

"Bend down, palm. Bend down, palm."

But what was this, what could this be? The palm-leaves rustled, as if a hurricane rushed through them, and shudder upon shudder passed through the tall stem. And the palm felt that the little one was the stronger. It could not resist him.

And with its high stem it bowed down before the child, as men bow down before princes. In a mighty arch it lowered itself towards earth, and at last bowed so low that its great crown of trembling leaves swept the sand of the desert.

The child did not seem to be either frightened or surprised, but with a joyous exclamation it ran and plucked one cluster after another from the crown of the old palm.

When the child had gathered enough, and the tree was still lying on the earth, he again went to it, stroked it, and said in his gentlest voice:

"Arise, palm, arise."

And the great tree raised itself silently and obediently on its stem, whilst the leaves played like harps.

"Now I know for whom they play the death-song," the old palm said to itself, when it again stood erect. "It is not for any of these strangers."

But the man and woman knelt down on their knees and praised God.

"Thou hast seen our fear and taken it from us. Thou art the Mighty One, that bends the stem of the palm like a reed. Of whom should we be afraid when Thy strength protects us?"

Next time a caravan passed through the desert, one of the travellers saw that the crown of the great palm had withered.

"How can that have happened?" said the traveller. "Have we not heard that this palm should not die before it had seen a King greater than Solomon?"

"Perhaps it has seen Him," answered another wanderer of the desert.

THE HAUGHTY ASPEN

A German Legend

NORA ARCHIBALD SMITH

As I went through the tangled wood
  I heard the Aspen shiver.
"What dost thou ail, sweet Aspen, say,
  Why do thy leaflets quiver?"

"'Twas long ago," the Aspen sighed—
  How long is past my knowing—
"When Mary Mother rode adown
  This wood where I was growing.
Blest Joseph journey'd by her side,
  Upon his good staff resting,
And in her arms the Heav'nly Babe,
  Dove of the World, was nesting.
Fair was the mother, shining-fair,
  A lily sweetly blowing;
The Babe was but a lily-bud,
  Like to his mother showing.

The birds began, 'Thy Master comes!
  Bow down, bow down before Him!'
The date, the fig, the hazel tree,
In rev'rence bent to adore Him.
I only, out of all the host
  Of bird and tree and flower,—
I, haughty, would not bow my head,
  Nor own my Master's power.
'Proud Aspen,' quoth the Mother-Maid,

'Thy Lord, dost thou defy Him?
When emperors worship at His shrine,
  Wilt courtesy deny Him?'
I heard her voice; my heart was rent,
  My boughs began to shiver,
And age on age, in punishment,
  My sorrowing leaflets quiver."

Still in the dark and tangled wood,
  Still doth the Aspen quiver.
The haughty tree doth bear a curse,
  Her leaflets aye must shiver.

THE LITTLE MUD-SPARROWS

Jewish Legend

ELIZABETH STUART PHELPS

I like that old, kind legend
  Not found in Holy Writ,
And wish that John or Matthew
  Had made Bible out of it.

But though it is not Gospel,
  There is no law to hold
The heart from growing better
  That hears the story told:—

How the little Jewish children
  Upon a summer day,
Went down across the meadows
  With the Child Christ to play.

And in the gold-green valley,
  Where low the reed-grass lay,

They made them mock mud-sparrows
  Out of the meadow clay.

So, when these all were fashioned,
  And ranged in rows about,
"Now," said the little Jesus,
  "We'll let the birds fly out."

Then all the happy children
  Did call, and coax, and cry—

Each to his own mud-sparrow:
  "Fly, as I bid you! Fly!"

But earthen were the sparrows,
  And earth they did remain,
Though loud the Jewish children
  Cried out, and cried again.

Except the one bird only
  The little Lord Christ made;
The earth that owned Him Master,
  —His earth heard and obeyed.

Softly He leaned and whispered:
  "Fly up to Heaven! Fly!"
And swift, His little sparrow
  Went soaring to the sky,

And silent, all the children
  Stood, awestruck, looking on,
Till, deep into the heavens,
  The bird of earth had gone.

I like to think, for playmate
  We have the Lord Christ still,
And that still above our weakness
  He works His mighty will,

That all our little playthings
  Of earthen hopes and joys
Shall be, by His commandment,
  Changed into heavenly toys.

Our souls are like the sparrows
   Imprisoned in the clay,
Bless Him who came to give them wings
   Upon a Christmas Day!

THE CHILDREN OF WIND AND THE CLAN OF PEACE

FIONA MACLEOD

I will tell this Legend as simply but also with what beauty I can, because the words of the old Highland woman, who told it to me,...though simple were beautiful with ancient idiom.

We must go back near twenty hundred years.... It was in the last month of the last year of the seven years' silence and peace: the seventh year in the mortal life of Jesus the Christ. It was on the twenty-fifth day of that month, the day of His holy birth.

It was a still day. The little white flowers that were called Breaths of Hope and that we now call Stars of Bethlehem were so hushed in quiet that the shadows of moths lay on them like the dark motionless violet in the hearts of pansies. In the long swards of tender grass the multitude of the daisies were white as milk faintly stained with flusht dews fallen from roses. On the meadows of white poppies were long shadows blue as the blue lagoons of the sky among drifting snow-white moors of cloud. Three white aspens on the pastures were in a still sleep: their tremulous leaves made no rustle, though there was a soundless wavering fall of little dusky shadows, as in the dark water of a pool where birches lean in the yellow hour of the frostfire. Upon the pastures were ewes and lambs sleeping, and yearling kids opened and closed their onyx eyes among the garths of white clover.

It was the Sabbath, and Jesus walked alone. When He came to a little rise in the grass He turned and looked back at the house where His parents dwelled. Joseph sat on a bench, with bent shoulders, and was dreaming with fixt gaze into the west, as seamen stare across the interminable wave at the pale green horizons that are like the grassy shores of home. Mary was standing, dressed in long white raiment, white as a lily, with her right hand shading her eyes as she looked to the east, dreaming her dream.

The young Christ sighed, but with the love of all love in His heart. "So shall it be till the day of days," He said aloud; "even so shall the hearts of men dwell among shadows and glories, in the West of passing things: even so shall that which is immortal turn to the East and watch for the coming of Joy through the Gates of Life."

At the sound of His voice He heard a sudden noise as of many birds, and turned and looked beyond the low upland where He stood. A pool of pure water lay in the hollow, fed by a ceaseless wellspring, and round it and over it circled birds whose breasts were grey as pearl and whose necks shone purple and grass-green and rose. The noise was of their wings, for though the birds were beautiful they were voiceless and dumb as flowers.

At the edge of the pool stood two figures, whom He knew to be of the angelic world because of their beauty, but who had on them the illusion of mortality so that the child did not know them. But He saw that one was beautiful as Night, and one beautiful as Morning.

He drew near.

"I have lived seven years," He said, "and I wish to send peace to the far ends of the world."

"Tell your secret to the birds," said one.

"Tell your secret to the birds," said the other.

So Jesus called to the birds.

"Come," He cried; and they came.

Seven came flying from the left, from the side of the angel beautiful as Night. Seven came flying from the right, from the side of the angel beautiful as Morning.

To the first He said: "Look into my heart."

But they wheeled about Him, and with newfound voices mocked, crying, "How could we see into your heart that is hidden" ... and mocked and derided, crying, "What is Peace! ... Leave us alone! Leave us alone!"

So Christ said to them:

"I know you for the birds of Ahriman, who is not beautiful but is Evil. Henceforth ye shall be black as night, and be children of the winds."

To the seven other birds which circled about Him, voiceless, and brushing their wings against His arms, He cried:

"Look into my heart."

And they swerved and hung before Him in a maze of wings, and looked into His pure heart: and, as they looked, a soft murmurous sound came from them, drowsy-sweet, full of peace: and as they hung there like a breath in frost they became white as snow.

"Ye are the Doves of the Spirit," said Christ, "and to you I will commit that which ye have seen. Henceforth shall your plumage be white and your voices be the voices of peace."

The young Christ turned, for He heard Mary calling to the sheep and goats, and knew that dayset was come and that in the valleys the gloaming was already rising like smoke from the urns of the twilight. When He looked back He saw by the pool neither the Son of Joy nor the Son of Sorrow, but seven white doves were in the cedar beyond the pool, cooing in low ecstasy of peace and awaiting through sleep and dreams the rose-red pathways of the dawn. Down the long grey reaches of the ebbing day He saw seven birds rising and falling on the wind, black as black water in caves, black as the darkness of night in old pathless woods.

And that is how the first doves became white, and how the first crows became black and were called by a name that means the clan of darkness, the children of the wind.

THE CHILD JESUS IN THE GARDEN

AUTHOR UNKNOWN

Cold was the day, when in a garden bare,
  Walked the Child Jesus, wrapt in holy thought;
His brow seemed clouded with a weight of care;
  Calmness and rest from worldly things he sought.

Soon was his presence missed within his home;
  His mother gently marked his every way;
Forth then she came to seek where he did roam.
  Full of sweet words his trouble to allay.

Through chilling snow she toiled to reach his side,
  Forcing her way mid branches brown and sere,
Hastening that she his sorrows might divide,
  Share all his woe, or calm his gloomy fear.

Sweet was her face, as o'er his head she bent,
  Longing to melt his look of saddest grief.
With lifted eyes, his ear to her he lent;
  Her kindly solace brought his soul relief.

Then did he smile—a smile of love so deep,
  Winter himself grew warm beneath its glow;
From drooping branches scented blossoms peep;
  Up springs the grass; the sealèd fountains flow.

Summer and spring did with each other vie,
  Offering to Him the fragrance of their store;
Chanting sweet notes, the birds around him fly,
  Wondering why earth had checkered so her floor.

THE MYSTIC THORN

ADAPTED FROM TRADITIONAL SOURCES

"Three hawthornes also that groweth in Werall
Do burge and bere grene leaves at Christmas
As fresshe as other in May."

It was Christmas day in the year 63. The autumn colors of red and gold
had long since faded from the hills, and the trees which covered the island
valley of Glastonbury, the Avalon or Apple-tree isle of the early Britons,
were bare and leafless. The spreading, glass-like waters encircling it
round about gleamed faintly in the pale afternoon light of the winter's
day. The light fell also on the silver stems of the willows and on the tall
flags and bending reeds and osiers which bordered the marsh island.
Westward the long ranges of hills running seaward were purple in the
distance and their tops were partly hidden by the misty white clouds
which rested lightly upon them. To the south rose sharply and abruptly a
high, pointed hill, the tor of Glastonbury.

It was nearing the sunset hour when a little band of men in pilgrim
garb, approaching from the west and climbing the long, hilly ridge,
came within sight of this "isle of rest." Twelve pilgrims there were in all,
in dress and appearance very unlike the fair-haired Britons who at that
time dwelt in the land. One, he who led the way, was an old man. His
hair was white and his long, white beard fell upon his breast, but he was
tall and erect and bore no other signs of age. In his hand he carried a
stout hawthorn staff.

The men were climbing slowly up the hill, for they were all weary with
long travelling. And here at the summit of the ridge they stopped to look
out over the wooded hills, the wide-spreading waters and the grassy
island with its leafless thickets of oak and alder. Sitting down to rest,

they spoke one to another of their long journeying from the far-distant land of Palestine and of their hope that here their pilgrimage might have end.

Those who were with him called their leader Joseph of Arimathea. He it was who had been known among the Jews many years before as a counsellor, "a good man, and a just," and who, when the Saviour was crucified on Calvary, had given his sepulchre to receive the body of the Lord.

From this tomb upon the third day came the risen Saviour; but the people, thinking that Joseph had stolen away the body, seized and imprisoned him in a chamber where there was no window. They fastened the door and put a seal upon the lock and placed men before the door to guard it. Then the priests and the Levites contrived to what death they should put him; but when they sent for Joseph to be brought forth he could not be found, though the seal was still upon the lock and the guard before the door.

The disciples of Joseph as they gathered about their fire of an evening often told how, at night, as he prayed, the prison chamber had been filled with a light brighter than that of the sun, and Jesus himself had appeared to him and had led him forth unharmed to his own house in Arimathea.

And sometimes they told how, again imprisoned, he had been fed from the Holy Cup from which the Saviour had drunk at the "last sad supper with his own" and in which Joseph had caught the blood of his Master when he was on the cross, and how he had been blest with such heavenly visions that the years passed and seemed to him as naught.

Now after a certain time he had been released from prison; but there were people who still doubted him and so with his friends, Lazarus and Mary Magdalene and Philip and others, he had been driven away from Jerusalem. The small vessel, without oars, rudder or sail, in which they had been cast adrift on the Mediterranean, had come at last in safety to the coast of Gaul. And for many years since then had Joseph wandered through the land carrying ever with him two precious relics, the Holy Grail and "that same spear wherewith the Roman pierced the side of Christ." Now at last with a chosen band of disciples he had reached the little-known island of the Britons.

Landing from their little boat in the early morn on this unknown coast, they had knelt upon the shore while Joseph "gave blessing to the God of heaven in a lowly chanted prayer." Then, "over the brow of the seaward hill" they had passed, led by an invisible hand and singing as they went. All day through dark forests and over reedy swamps they had made their way and now at nightfall, tired and wayworn, they rested on the ridgy hill which has ever since been known by the name of Wearyall.

During the long day's march they had seen but few of the people of the land and these had held aloof.

Now, suddenly, the silence was broken by loud cries and shouts, and groups of the native Britons, wild and uncouth in appearance, their half-naked bodies stained blue with woad, were seen coming from different directions up the hill. They were armed with spears, hatchets of bronze, and other rude weapons of olden warfare and, as they came rapidly nearer, their threatening aspect and menacing cries startled the pilgrim band. Rising hastily, as though they would flee, the men looked in terror, one toward another. Joseph alone showed no trace of fear and, obedient to a sign from him, they all knelt in prayer upon the hillside.

Then, thrusting his thorny staff into the ground beside him and raising both hands toward heaven, Joseph claimed possession of this new land in the name of his Master, Christ.

"'This staff hath borne me long and well,'
Then spake that saint divine,

'Over mountain and over plain,
On quest of the Promise-sign;
For aye let it stand in this western land,
And God do no more to me
If there ring not out from this realm about,
Tibi gloria, Domine.'"

His voice ceased and the men rose from their knees, looking expectantly for the heavenly sign, but ready, if need be, to meet with courage the threatened attack.

But stillness had again settled over the hill. Only a few rods distant the Britons had stopped and grouped closely together were gazing in awestruck silence upon the dry and withered staff, which had so often aided Joseph in his wanderings from the Holy Land. Following their gaze, Joseph and his companions turned toward it and even as they did so, behold! A miracle! The staff took root and grew and, as they watched, they saw it put forth branches and green leaves, fair buds and milk-white blossoms which filled the air with their sweet odor.

For a moment, awed and amazed, all stood silent. Wondrously had Joseph's prayer been answered! This was indeed the heavenly token which had been foretold! Then with tears of joy all cried out as with one voice, "Our God is with us! Jesus is with us!"

Marvelling much at the strange things they had just seen and heard, the Britons dropped their weapons and fled in haste from the hill.

Then did Joseph and his disciples go down across the marsh into the valley and there they rested undisturbed.

Word of the miracle which had thus been wrought on Wearyall Hill was brought soon to Arviragus, the heathen king of the time, and he welcomed gladly the holy men and gave them the beautiful vale of

Avalon whereon to live. There they built "a little lonely church," with roof of rushes and walls of woven twigs and "wattles from the marsh," the first Christian church which had ever been built in Britain.

There they dwelt for many years, serving God, fasting and praying, and there Joseph taught the half-barbarous Britons, who gathered to listen to him, the faith of Christ.

* * * * *

Time passed and the little, low, wattled church became a great and beautiful abbey. Many pilgrims there were who came to worship at the shrine of St. Joseph; to drink from the holy well which sprang from the foot of Chalice Hill where the Holy Cup lay buried; and to watch the budding of the mystic thorn, which, year after year, when the snows of Christmas covered the hills, put forth its holy blossoms, "a symbol of God's promise, care and love."

Now long, long afterward there came a time when there was war in the land and one day a rough soldier who recked not of its heavenly origin cut down the sacred tree. Only a flat stone now marks the place where it once stood and where Joseph's staff burst into bloom. But there were other trees which had been grown from slips of the miraculous thorn and these, "mindful of our Lord" still keep the sacred birthday and blossom each year on Christmas Day.

THE BLOOMING OF THE WHITE THORN

EDITH MATILDA THOMAS

God shield ye, comrades of the road!
  And while our way we hold,
List while I tell how it first befell
  In the wondrous days of old.

* * * * *

From off the sea, the pilgrims came,
  With sea-toil wracked and worn;
The air blew keen, and the frost was sheen,
  Upon that wintry morn.

Through Glastonbury street went they;
  And ever on, and on,
Till they pass the well of the fairy spell,
  And the oak of Avalon.

They hear the rustling leaves and few,
  That linger on the bough;
But still they fare through the bitter air,
  And climb a hill-slope now.

On Weary-All-Hill their feet they stay
  (Full well that Hill ye know);
There may they rest, by toil oppressed,
  While round them drops the snow.

And one—far gone in age was he—
  As snow, his locks were white—

The staff of thorn which he had borne,
  Did plant upon that height.

A thorn-stick dry, that pilgrim staff,
  He set it in the ground:
And, swift as sight, with blossoms white
  The branching staff was crowned!

Each year since then (if sooth men say)
  Upon this Blessed Morn,
Who climbs that Hill, may see at will
  The flower upon the thorn!

Howe'er the wind may drive the sleet,
  That thorn will blooming be;
And some have seen a fair Child lean
  From out that blossomed tree!

One moment only—then, apace,
  Both flower and leaf are shorn;
And, gaunt and chill, on Weary-All-Hill,
  There stands an ancient thorn!

God shield ye, comrades of the road—
  With grace your spirits fill,
That ye may see the White-thorn tree
  A-bloom on Weary-All-Hill!

LEGEND OF ST. CHRISTOPHER

ADAPTED FROM THE GOLDEN LEGEND

There was a mighty man of old who dwelt in the land of Canaan. Large was he and tall of stature and stronger than any man whom the world had ever seen. Therefore was he called Offero, or, "The Bearer." Now he served the king of Canaan, but he was proud of his great strength and upon a time it came in his mind that he would seek the greatest king who then reigned and him only would he serve and obey.

So he travelled from one country to another until at length he came to one where ruled a powerful king whose fame was great in all the land.

"Thou art the conqueror of nations?" asked Offero.

"I am," replied the king.

"Then take me into your service, for I will serve none but the mightiest of earth."

"That then am I," returned the king, "for truly I fear none."

So the king received Offero into his service and made him to dwell in his court.

But once at eventide a minstrel sang before the king a merry song in which he named oft the evil one. And every time that the king heard the name of Satan he grew pale and hastily made the sign of the cross upon his forehead. Offero marvelled thereat and demanded of the king the meaning of the sign and wherefore he thus crossed himself. And because the king would not tell him Offero said, "If thou tell me not, I shall no longer dwell with thee." Then the king answered, saying, "Always when I hear Satan named, I fear that he may have power over me and therefore I make this sign that he harm me not."

"Who is Satan?" asked Offero.

"He is a wicked monarch," replied the king, "wicked but powerful."

"More powerful than thou art?"

"Aye, verily."

"And fearest thou that he hurt thee?"

"That do I, and so do all."

"Then," cried Offero, "is he more mighty and greater than thou art. I will go seek him. Henceforth he shall be my master for I would fain serve the mightiest and the greatest lord of all the world."

So Offero departed from the king and sought Satan. Everywhere he met people who had given themselves over to his rule and at last one day as he was crossing a wide desert he saw a great company of knights approaching. One of them, mounted upon a great black horse, came to him and demanded whither he went, and Offero made answer, "I seek Satan, for he is mighty, and I would fain serve him."

Then returned the knight, "I am he whom thou seekest."

When Offero heard these words he was right glad and took Satan to be his lord and master.

This king was indeed powerful and a long time did Offero serve him, but it chanced one day as they were journeying together they came to a place where four roads met and in the midst of the space stood a little cross. As soon as Satan saw the cross he was afraid and turned quickly aside and fled toward the desert. Offero followed him marvelling much at the sight. And after, when they had come back to the highway they had left, he inquired of Satan why he was thus troubled and had gone so far out of his way to avoid the cross. But Satan answered him not a word.

Then Offero said to him, "If thou wilt not tell me, I shall depart from thee straightway and shall serve thee no more."

"Know then," said Satan, "there was a man called Christ who suffered on the cross and whenever I see his sign I am sore afraid and flee from it, lest he destroy me."

"If then thou art afraid of his sign," cried Offero, "he is greater and more mighty than thou, and I see well that I have labored in vain, for I have not found the greatest lord of the world. I will serve thee no longer. Go thy way alone, for I will go to seek Christ."

And when he had long sought and demanded where he should find Him, he came at length into a great desert where dwelt a hermit, a servant of the Christ. The hermit told him of the Master whom he was seeking and said to him, "This king whom thou dost wish to serve is not an earthly ruler and he requireth that thou oft fast and make many prayers."

But Offero understood not the meaning of worship and prayer and he answered, "Require of me some other thing and I shall do it, but I know naught of this which thou requirest."

Then the hermit said to him, "Knowest thou the river, a day's journey from here, where there is neither ford nor bridge and many perish and are lost? Thou art large and strong. Therefore go thou and dwell by this river and bear over all who desire to cross its waters. That is a service which will be well pleasing to the Christ whom thou desirest to serve, and sometime, if I mistake not, he whom thou seekest will come to thee."

Offero was right joyful at these words and answered, "This service may I well do."

So he hastened to the river and upon its banks he built himself a little hut of reeds. He bare a great pole in his hand to sustain him in the water and many weary wayfarers did he help to cross the turbulent stream. So he lived a long time, bearing over all manner of people without ceasing, and still he saw nothing of the Christ.

Now it happened one night that a storm was raging and the river was very high. Tired with his labors, Offero had just flung himself down on his rude bed to sleep when he heard the voice of a child which called him and said, "Offero, Offero, come out and bear me over."

Offero arose and went out from his cabin, but in the darkness he could see no one. And when he was again in the house, he heard the same voice and he ran out again and found no one. A third time he heard the call and going out once more into the storm, there upon the river bank he found a fair young child who besought him in pleading tones, "Wilt thou not carry me over the river this night, Offero?"

The strong man gently lifted the child on his shoulders, took his staff and stepped into the stream. And the water of the river arose and swelled more and more and the child was heavy as lead. And alway as he went farther, higher and higher swelled the waters and the child more and more waxed heavy, insomuch that he feared that they would both be drowned. Already his strength was nearly gone, but he thought of his Master whom he had not yet seen, and staying his footsteps with his palm staff struggled with all his might to reach the opposite shore. As at last he climbed the steep bank, suddenly the storm ceased and the waters calmed.

He set the child down upon the shore, saying, "Child, thou hast put me in great peril. Had I carried the whole world on my shoulders, the weight had not been greater. I might bear no greater burden."

"Offero," answered the child, "Marvel not, but rejoice; for thou hast borne not only all the world upon thee, but thou hast borne him that created and made all the world upon thy shoulders. I am Christ the king whom thou servest in this work. And for a token, that thou mayst know what I say to be the truth, set thy staff in the earth by thy house and thou shalt see in the morning that it shall bear flowers and fruit." With these words the child vanished from Offero's sight.

But Offero did even as he was bidden and set his staff in the earth and when he arose on the morrow, he found it like a palm-tree bearing flowers and leaves and clusters of dates. Then he knew that it was indeed Christ whom he had borne through the waters and he rejoiced that he had found his Master. From that day he served Christ faithfully and was no more called Offero, but Christopher, the Christ bearer.

ST. CHRISTOPHER OF THE GAEL

FIONA MACLEOD

Behind the wattle-woven house
Nial the Mighty gently crept
From out a screen of ashtree boughs
To where a captive white-robe slept.

Lightly he moved, as though ashamed;
To right and left he glanced his fears.
Nial the Mighty was he named
Though but an untried youth in years—

But tall he was, as tall as he,
White Dermid of the magic sword,
Or Torcall of the Hebrid Sea
Or great Cuhoolin of the Ford;

Strong as the strongest, too, he was:
As Balor of the Evil Eye;
As Fionn who kept the Ulster Pass
From dawn till blood-flusht sunset sky.

Much had he pondered all that day
The mystery of the men who died
On crosses raised along the way,
And perished singing side by side.

Modred the chief had sailed the Moyle,
Had reached Iona's guardless-shore,
Had seized the monks when at their toil
And carried northward, bound, a score.

Some he had thrust into the deep,
To see if magic fins would rise:
Some from high rocks he forced to leap,
To see wings fall from out the skies:

Some he had pinned upon tall spears,
Some tossed on shields with brazen clang,
To see if through their blood and tears
Their god would hear the hymns they sang.

But when his oarsmen flung their oars,
And laughed to see across the foam
The glimmer of the highland shores
And smoke-wreaths of the hidden home,

Modred was weary of his sport.
All day he brooded as he strode
Betwixt the reef-encircled port
And the oak-grove of the Sacred Road.

At night he bade his warriors raise
Seven crosses where the foamswept strand
Lay still and white beyond the blaze
Of the hundred camp-fires of the land.

The women milked the late-come kye,
The children raced in laughing glee;
Like sheep from out the fold of the sky
Stars leapt and stared at earth and sea.

At times a wild and plaintive air
Made delicate music far away:
A hill-fox barked before its lair:
The white owl hawked its shadowy prey.

But at the rising of the moon
The druids came from grove and glen,
And to the chanting of a rune
Crucified St. Columba's men.

They died in silence side by side,
But first they sang the evening hymn:
By midnight all but one had died,
At dawn he too was grey and grim.

One monk alone had Modred kept,
A youth with hair of golden-red,
Who never once had sighed or wept,
Not once had bowed his proud young head.

Broken he lay, and bound with thongs.
Thus had he seen his brothers toss
Like crows transfixed upon great prongs,
Till death crept up each silent cross.

Night grew to dawn, to scarlet morn;
Day waned to firelit, star-lit night:
But still with eyes of passionate scorn
He dared the worst of Modred's might.

When from the wattle-woven house
Nial the Mighty softly stepped,
And peered beneath the ashtree boughs
To where he thought the white-robe slept,

He heard the monk's words rise in prayer.
He heard a hymn's ascending breath—
"Christ, Son of God, to Thee I fare
This night upon the wings of death."

Nial the Mighty crossed the space,
He waited till the monk had ceased;
Then, leaning o'er the foam-white face,
He stared upon the dauntless priest.

"Speak low," he said, "and tell me this:
Who is the king you hold so great?—
Your eyes are dauntless flames of bliss
Though Modred taunts you with his hate:—

"This god or king, is He more strong
Than Modred is? And does He sleep
That thus your death-in-life is long,
And bonds your aching body keep?"

The monk's eyes stared in Nial's eyes:
"Young giant with a child's white heart,
I see a cross take shape and rise,
And thou upon it nailèd art!"

Nial looked back: no cross he saw
Looming from out the dreadful night:
Yet all his soul was filled with awe,
A thundercloud with heart of light.

"Tell me thy name," he said, "and why
Thou waitest thus the druid knife,
And carest not to live or die?
Monk, hast thou little care of life?"

"Great care of that I have," he said,
And looked at Nial with eyes of fire:
"My life begins when I am dead,
There only is my heart's desire."

Nial the Mighty sighed. "Thy words
Are as the idle froth of foam,
Or clashing of triumphant swords
When Modred brings the foray home.

"My name is Nial: Nial the Strong:
A lad in years, but as you see
More great than heroes of old song
Or any lordly men that be.

"To Modred have I come from far,
O'er many a hill and strath and stream.
To be a mighty sword in war,
And this because I dreamed a dream:

"My dream was that my strength so great
Should serve the greatest king there is:
Modred the Pict thus all men rate,
And so I sought this far-off Liss.

"But if there be a greater yet,
A king or god whom he doth fear,
My service he shall no more get,
My strength shall rust no longer here."

The monk's face gladdened. "Go, now, go;
To Modred go: he sitteth dumb,
And broods on what he fain would know:
And say, 'O King, the Cross is come!'

"Then shall the king arise in wrath,
And bid you go from out his sight,
For if he meet you on his path
He'll leave you stark and still and white.

"Thus shall he show, great king and all,
He fears the glorious Cross of Christ,
And dreads to hear slain voices call
For vengeance on the sacrificed.

"But, Nial, come not here again:
Long before dawn my soul shall be
Beyond the reach of any pain
That Modred dreams to prove on me.

"Go forth thyself at dawn, and say
'This is Christ's holy natal morn,
My king is He from forth this day
When He to save mankind was born':

"Go forth and seek a lonely place
Where a great river fills the wild;
There bide, and let thy strength be grace,
And wait the Coming of a Child.

"A wondrous thing shall then befall:
And when thou seek'st if it be true,
Green leaves along thy staff shall crawl,
With, flowers of every lovely hue."

The monk's face whitened, like sea-foam:
Seaward he stared, and sighed "I go—
Farewell—my Lord Christ calls me home!"
Nial stooped and saw death's final throe.

An hour before the dawn he rose
And sought out Modred, brooding, dumb;
"O King," he said, "my bond I close,
King Christ I seek: the Cross is come!"

Swift as a stag's leap from a height
King Modred drew his dreadful sword:
Then as a snow-wraith, silent, white,
He stared and passed without a word.

Before the flush of dawn was red
A druid came to Nial the Great:
"The doom of death hath Modred said,
Yet fears this Christ's mysterious hate:

"So get you hence, you giant-thewed man:
Go your own way: come not again:
No more are you of Modred's clan:
Go now, forthwith, lest you be slain."

Nial went forth with gladsome face;
No more of Modred's clan he was:
"Now, now," he cried, "Christ's trail I'll trace,
And nowhere turn, and nowhere pause."

He laughed to think how Modred feared
The wrath of Christ, the monk's white king:
"A greater than Modred hath appeared,
To Him my sword and strength I bring."

All day, all night, he walked afar:
He saw the moon rise white and still:
The evening and the morning star:
The sunrise burn upon the hill.

He heard the moaning of the seas,
The vast sigh of the sunswept plain,
The myriad surge of forest-trees;
Saw dusk and night return again.

At falling of the dusk he stood
Upon a wild and desert land:
Dark fruit he gathered for his food,
Drank water from his hollowed hand,

Cut from an ash a mighty bough
And trimmed and shaped it to the half:
"Safe in the desert am I now,
With sword," he said, "and with this staff."

The stars came out: Arcturus hung
His ice-blue fire far down the sky:
The Great Bear through the darkness swung:
The Seven Watchers rose on high.

A great moon flooded all the west.
Silence came out of earth and sea
And lay upon the husht world's breast,
And breathed mysteriously.

Three hours Nial walked, three hours and more:
Then halted when beyond the plain
He stood upon that river's shore
The dying monk had bid him gain.

A little house he saw: clay-wrought,
Of wattle woven through and through:
Then, all his weariness forgot,
The joy of drowning-sleep he knew.

Three hours he slept, and then he heard
A voice—and yet a voice so low
It might have been a dreaming bird
Safe-nested by the rushing flow.

Almost he slept once more: then, *Hush!*
Once more he heard above the noise
And tempest of the river's rush
The thin faint words of a child's voice.

"Good Sir, awake from sleep and dream,
Good Sir, come out and carry me
Across this dark and raging stream
Till safe on the other side I be."

Great Nial shivered on his bed:
"No human creature calls this night,
It is a wild fetch of the dead,"
He thought, and shrunk, and shook with fright.

Once more he heard that infant-cry:
"Come out, Good Sir, or else I drown—
Come out, Good Sir, or else I die
And you, too, lose a golden crown."

"A golden crown"—so Nial thought—
"No—no—not thus shall I be ta'en!
Keep, ghost-of-the-night, your crown gold-wrought—
Of sleep and peace I am full fain!"

Once more the windy dark was filled
With lonely cry, with sobbing plaint:
Nial's heart grew sore, its fear was stilled,
King Christ, he knew, would scorn him faint.

"Up, up thou coward, thou sluggard, thou,"
He cried, and sprang from off his bed—
"No crown thou seekest for thy brow,
But help for one in pain and dread!"

Out in the wide and lonely dark
No fetch he saw, no shape, no child:
Almost he turned again—but *hark!*
A song rose o'er the waters wild:

A king am I
Tho' a little Child,
Son of God am I,
Meek and mild,
Beautiful
Because God hath said
Let my cup be full
Of wine and bread.

Come to me
Shaken heart,
Shaken heart!
I will not flee.
My heart
Is thy heart
O shaken heart!
Stoop to my Cup,
Sup,
Drink of the wine:
The wine and the bread,
Saith God,
Are mine—
My Flesh and my Blood!

Throw thy sword in the flood:
Come, shaken heart:
Fearful thou art!
Have no more fear—

Lo, I am here,
The little One,
The Son,
Thy Lord and thy King.

It is I who sing:
Christ, your King....
Be not afraid:
Look, I am Light,
A great star
Seen from afar
In the darkness of night:
I am Light,
Be not afraid ...
Wade, wade
Into the deep flood!
Think of the Bread,
The Wine and the Bread
That are my Flesh and Blood,
Cross, cross the Flood,
Sure is the goal ...
Be not afraid
O Soul,
Be not afraid!

Nial's heart was filled with joy and pain:
"This is my king, my king indeed:
To think that drown'd in sleep I've lain
When Christ the Child-God crieth in need!"

Swift from his wattled hut he strode,
Stumbling among the grass and bent,

And, seeking where the river flowed,
Far o'er the dark flood peered and leant:

Then suddenly beside him saw
A little Child all clad in white:
He bowed his head in love and awe,
Then lifted high his burthen light.

High on his shoulders sat the Child,
While with strong limbs he fared among
The rushing waters black and wild
And where the fiercest currents swung.

The waters rose more high, more high,
Higher and higher every yard ...
Nial stumbled on with sob and sigh,
Christ heard him panting sore and hard.

"O Child," Nial cried, "forbear, forbear!
Hark you not how these waters whirled!
The weight of all the earth I bear,
The weary weight of all the world!"

"*Christopher!*" ... low above the noise,
The rush, the darkness, Nial heard
The far-off music of a Voice
That said all things in saying one word—

"Christopher ... this thy name shall be!
Christ-bearer is thy name, even so
Because of service done to me
Heavy with weight of the world's woe."

With breaking sobs, with panting breath
Christopher grasped a bent-held dune,
Then with flung staff and as in death
Forward he fell in a heavy swoon.

All night he lay in silence there,
But safe from reach of surging tide:
White angels had him in their care,
Christ healed and watched him side by side.

When all the silver wings of dawn
Had waved above the rose-flusht east,
Christopher woke ... his dream was gone.
The angelic songs had ceased.

Was it a dream in very deed,
He wondered, broken, trembling, dazed?
His staff he lifted from the mead
And as an upright sapling raised.

Lo, it was as the monk had said—
If he would prove the vision true,
His staff would blossom to its head
With flowers of every lovely hue.

Christopher bowed: before his eyes
Christ's love fulfilled the holy hour....
A south-wind blew, green leaves did rise
And the staff bloomed a myriad flower!

Christopher bowed in holy prayer,
While Christ's love fell like healing dew:
God's father-hand was on him there:
The peace of perfect peace he knew.

THE CROSS OF THE DUMB

A Christmas on Iona, Long, Long Ago

FIONA MACLEOD

One eve, when St. Columba strode
In solemn mood along the shore,
He met an angel on the road
Who but a poor man's semblance bore.

He wondered much, the holy saint,
What stranger sought the lonely isle,
But seeing him weary and wan and faint
St. Colum hailed him with a smile.

"Remote our lone Iona lies
Here in the grey and windswept sea,
And few are they whom my old eyes
Behold as pilgrims bowing the knee....

"But welcome ... welcome ... stranger-guest,
And come with me and you shall find
A warm and deer-skinn'd cell for rest
And at our board a welcome kind....

"Yet tell me ere the dune we cross
How came you to this lonely land?
No curraghs in the tideway toss
And none is beached upon the strand!"

The weary pilgrim raised his head
And looked and smiled and said, "From far,

My wandering feet have here been led
By the glory of a shining star...."

St. Colum gravely bowed, and said,
"Enough, my friend, I ask no more;
Doubtless some silence-vow was laid
Upon thee, ere thou sought'st this shore:

"Now, come: and doff this raiment sad
And those rough sandals from thy feet:
The holy brethren will be glad
To haven thee in our retreat."

Together past the praying cells
And past the wattle-woven dome
Whence rang the tremulous vesper bells
St. Colum brought the stranger home.

From thyme-sweet pastures grey with dews
The milch-cows came with swinging tails:
And whirling high the wailing mews
Screamed o'er the brothers at their pails.

A single spire of smoke arose,
And hung, a phantom, in the cold:
Three younger monks set forth to close
The ewes and lambs within the fold.

The purple twilight stole above
The grey-green dunes, the furrowed leas:
And Dusk, with breast as of a dove,
Brooded: and everywhere was peace.

Within the low refectory sate
The little clan of holy folk:
Then, while the brothers mused and ate,
The wayfarer arose and spoke....

"O Colum of Iona-Isle,
And ye who dwell in God's quiet place,
Before I crossed your narrow kyle
I looked in Heaven upon Christ's face."

Thereat St. Colum's startled glance
Swept o'er the man so poorly clad,
And all the brethren looked askance
In fear the pilgrim-guest was mad.

"And, Colum of God's Church i' the sea
And all ye Brothers of the Rood,
The Lord Christ gave a dream to me
And bade me bring it ye as food.

"Lift to the wandering cloud your eyes
And let them scan the wandering Deep....
Hark ye not there the wandering sighs
Of brethren ye as outcasts keep?"

Thereat the stranger bowed, and blessed;
Then, grave and silent, sought his cell:
St. Colum mused upon his guest,
Dumb wonder on the others fell.

At dead of night the Abbot came
To where the weary wayfarer slept:
"Tell me," he said, "thy holy name..."
—No more, for on bowed knees he wept....

Great awe and wonder fell on him;
His mind was like a lonely wild
When suddenly is heard a hymn
Sung by a little innocent child.

For now he knew their guest to be
No man as he and his, but one
Who in the Courts of Ecstasy
Worships, flame-winged, the Eternal Son.

The poor bare cell was filled with light,
That came from the swung moons the Seven
Seraphim swing day and night
Adown the infinite walls of Heaven.

But on the fern-wove mattress lay
No weary guest. St. Colum kneeled,
And found no trace; but, ashen-grey,
Far off he heard glad anthems pealed.

At sunrise when the matins-bell
Made a cold silvery music fall
Through silence of each lonely cell
And over every fold and stall,

St. Colum called his monks to come
And follow him to where his hands
Would raise the Great Cross of the Dumb
Upon the Holy Island's sands....

"For I shall call from out the Deep
And from the grey fields of the skies,
The brethren we as outcasts keep,
Our kindred of the dumb wild eyes....

"Behold, on this Christ's natal morn,
God wills the widening of His laws,
Another miracle to be born—
For lo, our guest an Angel was!...

"His Dream the Lord Christ gave to him
To bring to us as Christ-Day food,
That Dream shall rise a holy hymn
And hang like a flower upon the Rood!..."

Thereat, while all with wonder stared
St. Colum raised the Holy Tree:
Then all with Christ-Day singing fared
To where the last sands lipped the sea.

St. Colum raised his arms on high ...
"O ye, all creatures of the wing,
Come here from out the fields o' the sky,
Come, here and learn a wondrous thing!"

At that the wild clans of the air
Came sweeping in a mist of wings—
Ospreys and fierce solanders there,
Sea-swallows wheeling mazy rings,

The foam-white mew, the green-black scart,
The famishing hawk, the wailing tern,
All birds from the sand-building mart
To lonely bittern and heron....

St. Colum raised beseeching hands
And blessed the pastures of the sea:
"Come, all ye creatures, to the sands,
Come and behold the Sacred Tree!"

At that the cold clans of the wave
With spray and surge and splash appeared:
Up from each wrack-strewn, lightless cave
Dim day-struck eyes affrighted peered.

The pollacks came with rushing haste,
The great sea-cod, the speckled bass;
Along the foaming tideway raced
The herring-tribes like shimmering glass:

The mackerel and the dog-fish ran,
The whiting, haddock, in their wake:
The great sea-flounders upward span,
The fierce-eyed conger and the hake:

The greatest and the least of these
From hidden pools and tidal ways
Surged in their myriads from the seas
And stared at St. Columba's face.

"Hearken," he cried, with solemn voice—
"Hearken! ye people of the Deep,
Ye people of the skies, Rejoice!
No more your soulless terror keep!

"For lo, an Angel from the Lord
Hath shown us that wherein we sin—
But now we humbly do His Word
And call you, Brothers, kith and kin....

"No more we claim the world as ours
And everything that therein is—
To-day, Christ's Day, the infinite powers
Decree a common share of bliss.

"I know not if the new-waked soul
That stirs in every heart I see
Has yet to reach the far-off goal
Whose symbol is this Cross-shaped Tree....

"But, O dumb kindred of the skies,
O kinsfolk of the pathless seas,
All scorn and hate I exorcise,
And wish you nought but Love and Peace!"

* * * * *

Thus, on that Christmas-day of old
St. Colum broke the ancient spell.
A thousand years away have rolled,
'Tis now ... "a baseless miracle."

O fellow-kinsmen of the Deep,
O kindred of the wind and cloud,
God's children too ... how He must weep
Who on that day was glad and proud!

THE CHRISTMAS SONG OF CAEDMON

H.E.G. PARDEE

About the year 650, among the servants in the ancient Abbey of Streonschall, there was a cowherd whose name was Caedmon. The habits of the people of that age were simple and rude; their houses were comfortless huts, their dress was made from the skins of their flocks, or from animals taken in the chase; they had no books, and their literature was limited to the Latin manuscripts of the Church, which few of the monks even were learned enough to read, and fewer still to translate. Amid such influences, the life of a cowherd could scarcely be lifted above that of the beasts he cared for; if his hunger and thirst were satisfied, he would ask no more than a pleasant, daisied meadow in summer, and a warm nook in the winter. But Caedmon had a sensitive nature, that craved something nobler. When the minstrels struck their harps, and sung the wild traditions and fierce conflicts of their tribes and the guests followed with boisterous jest in their uncouth ballads, Caedmon sat silent and gloomy.

One evening, as the harp, passing from one to another, drew nearer him, dreading the oft-repeated taunts of his fellows, he crept away in the shadows, and went to his only bed,—a truss of straw.

After a while he slept, and in his sleep some one of lofty stature, and with kindly-beaming eyes, stood beside him, and commanded him to sing. "I cannot," replied Caedmon, despondingly.

"Sing!" was the uncompromising answer.

"What shall I sing?"

"The origin of all things."

Immediately before his quickened sense swept a vision of Creation, and to his glad surprise he described it all in song. The next morning he remembered, and repeated it; and the monks, hearing of it, took him into the monastery, and taught him scenes and sentences from the Bible, which he rendered into verse, and so became the first of the long line of sacred poets.

It was Christmas Eve, and the great hall of the Abbey was decked with the Druids' sacred mistletoe with its pearly fruitage, the bright green of the ivy, and branches of holly, with scarlet, shining berries. Great logs were heaped on the broad stones in the middle of the hall, and jets of flame leaped up to brighten the low, smoke-stained ceiling, and restless shadows flitted along the wall, while the smoke escaped through the opening in the roof, for chimneys were then, and for many centuries after, unknown. The unglazed windows were closed at nightfall by wooden shutters, and rude comfort cheered the inmates. A robin, who had fluttered in at dusk, and found Christmas cheer on the holly boughs and warmth for his numbed little feet, trilled a song of gratitude that winter had made such speed to be gone.

Two nights before, a company of pilgrims from the convents of Palestine, had come to the monastery. They had been many months on their way, eagerly welcomed wherever they stopped, for journeying was both difficult and dangerous, and travellers from such a remote region were rarely met. Their dark complexions, hair and beards; their bright, mobile expression; their manners toned by the graces of Eastern civilization, were a strange contrast to the shaggy, elfish, ruddy-faced throng about them. This Christmas Eve they were telling the monks wonderful stories of the Holy Land; its beautiful, vine-clad hills; its tropical, luscious fruits; its towering, plumy palms and hoary cedars; the long lines of caravans that wound over the silent, pathless deserts to bring to its cities the riches of Oriental commerce; the palaces and heathen temples of those cities, and the traditional glory of the Temple, with its magnificence of gold, and precious stones, and woods and ivory. On the table were huge platters of smoking meats, and serving men brought in flagons and tankards of ale, and feasting, stories and minstrelsy held the hours till the midnight bell called to the first mass and ushered in Christmas Day. Caedmon, coming back from the frosty chapel, saw the stars shining in the brilliance of winter skies. His heart was suffused with all he had heard the pilgrims repeat; for the first time it entered his mind that the same stars that he saw twinkling, held their course at that glad time when "the morning-stars sang together, and all the sons of God shouted for joy,"—a prelude to this other song of "the great multitude of the heavenly host." He entered the hall, and when the company reassembled, he took his harp, and sang with power and pathos of the slumbering flocks on Judea's upland pastures; the faithful, watching shepherds; the loneliness and silence of the night; the sudden, startling brightness that shone about them, and enveloped their angel visitant, who kindly soothed their alarm with "Fear not;" and the outburst of angelic song, unheard by the ears dulled with sleep, but overpowering these astonished men. "O happy shepherds! who alone among men, were ever privileged to hear the songs of heaven."

His audience was thrilled. Never had the monks heard Caedmon, or any other minstrel, sing with such fire; the intervening centuries fled before his song. They, too, went to the lowly manger, and saw the Divine Infant hushed on the happy breast of his young Mother and felt Mary's awe when the shepherds told her what they that night had seen and heard. While Caedmon sang they saw the caravan winding over an unmarked way and the wise men of the Orient following ever the strange star, till, after weeks of travel, it stood over the place where the young Child lay. They saw, too, the aged, bearded Melchior, Gaspar, young and fresh, and Balthazar the Moor, descend from their kneeling camels with their kingly offerings of gold, frankincense and myrrh and prostrate themselves in reverence before the Holy Babe.

"'Twas ages, ages long ago," and Caedmon and his hymns are nigh forgotten, but with each returning Christmas-tide may be heard again, as Caedmon heard of yore, the angels' song of joy: "Glory to God in the highest, and on earth peace, good will toward men."

GOOD KING WENCESLAS

JOHN MASON NEALE

Good King Wenceslas looked out
  On the Feast of Stephen,
When the snow lay round about,
  Deep, and crisp, and even.

Brightly shone the moon that night
  Though the frost was cruel,
When a poor man came in sight,
  Gath'ring winter fuel.

"Hither, page, and stand by me,
  If thou know'st it, telling,
Yonder peasant, who is he?
  Where and what his dwelling?"

"Sire, he lives a good league hence,
  Underneath the mountain;
Right against the forest fence,
  By Saint Agnes' fountain."

"Bring me flesh, and bring me wine,
  Bring me pine-logs hither;
Thou and I will see him dine,
  When we bear them thither."

Page and monarch, forth they went,
  Forth they went together;
Through the rude wind's wild lament
  And the bitter weather.

"Sire, the night is darker now,
  And the wind blows stronger;
Fails my heart, I know not how,
  I can go no longer."

"Mark my footsteps, good my page;
  Tread thou in them boldly:
Thou shalt find the winter rage
  Freeze thy blood less coldly."

In his master's steps he trod,
  Where the snow lay dinted;
Heat was in the very sod
  Which the saint had printed.

Therefore, Christian men, be sure,
  Wealth or rank possessing,
Ye who now will bless the poor,
  Shall yourselves find blessing.

THE CHRISTMAS AT GRECCIO: A STORY OF ST. FRANCIS

SOPHIE JEWETT

"The beautiful Mother is bending
  Low where her Baby lies
Helpless and frail, for her tending;
  But she knows the glorious eyes.

"The Mother smiles and rejoices
  While the Baby laughs in the hay;
She listens to heavenly voices:
  'The child shall be King, one day.'

"O dear little Christ in the manger,
  Let me make merry with Thee.
O King, in my hour of danger,
  Wilt Thou be strong for me?"

—Adapted from the Latin of Jacopone da Todi.
Thirteenth Century.

One night in December ... Brother Francis, with one companion, was walking through the beautiful valley of the Velino River, toward Rieti, a little city where he came often on his way from Assisi to Rome. To-night he had turned somewhat aside from the main road, for he wished to spend Christmas with his friend, Sir John of Greccio. Greccio is a tiny village, lying where the foothills begin, on the western side of the valley. The very feet of Brother Francis knew the road so well that he could have walked safely in the darkness, but it was not dark. The full moon floated over the valley, making the narrow river and the sharp outlines of the snow-covered mountains shine like silver. The plain and the lower hills were pasture land, and, not far from the road, on a grassy slope, the Brothers saw the red glow of an almost spent shepherds' fire. "Let us stop and visit our brothers, the shepherds," said Francis, and they turned toward the fading fire.

There was no sense of winter in the air, scarcely a touch of frost, and the only snow was that on the silver peaks against the sky. The shepherds, three men and one boy, lay sleeping soundly on the bare ground, with their sheepskin coats drawn closely around them. All about them the sheep were sleeping, too, but the solemn white sheep dogs were wide awake. If a stranger's foot had trod the grass never so softly, every dog would have barked, and every shepherd would have been on his feet in an instant. But the dogs trotted silently up to the Grey Brothers and rubbed against them, as if they said, "We are glad to see you again," for they knew the friendly feet of the Little Poor Man, and they had more than once helped him to eat the bread that was his only dinner. Followed by the dogs, Francis walked about among the shepherds, but they slept on, as only men who live out of doors can sleep, and Francis could not find it in his heart to waken them. The sheep lay huddled together in groups for more warmth. Around one small square of grass a net was stretched, and, inside it, were the mother sheep who had little lambs. There was no sound except the faint cry, now and then, of a baby lamb. The coals over which the shepherds had cooked their supper paled from dull red to grey, and there was only a thin column of smoke, white in the moonlight. Francis sat down on a stone, and the largest of the white dogs pressed up against his knee. Another went dutifully back to his post beside the fold where the mothers and babies slept. The Italian hillside seemed to Francis to change to that of Bethlehem, which he had seen, perhaps, on his Eastern journey; the clear December night seemed like that of the first Christmas Eve. "How these shepherds sleep!" he thought; "how they would awaken if they heard the 'Peace on earth' of the angels' song!" Then he remembered sadly how the armies that called themselves Christian had, year after year, battled with the Saracens over the cradle and the tomb of the Prince of Peace. The moonlight grew misty about him, the silver heights of the mountains and the silver line of the river faded, for the eyes of Brother Francis were full of tears.

As the two Brothers went on their way, Francis grew light of heart again. The sight of the shepherds sleeping on the grass had given him a new idea, and he was planning a surprise for his friends at Greccio. For at Greccio all were his friends, from Sir John, his host, down to the babies in the street. In the valley of Rieti he was almost as well known and as dearly loved as in his own valley of Assisi. The children of Greccio had never heard of Christmas trees, nor, perhaps, of Christmas presents. I am not sure that, in the thirteenth century, Italians had the beautiful custom which they now have of giving presents at Twelfth Night, in memory of the coming of the three kings with their gifts to the Christ Child; but in the thirteenth century, even as now, Christmas was the happiest festival of the year. This year all the folk of Greccio, big and little, were happier than usual because their beloved Brother Francis was to help them keep their Christmas-tide. Next day Francis confided his plan to his friend, Sir John, who promised that all should be ready on Christmas Eve.

On the day before Christmas, the people came from all the country around to see and hear Brother Francis. Men, women and children, dressed in their holiday clothes, walking, riding on donkeys, crowding into little carts drawn by great white oxen, from everywhere and in every fashion, the country folk came toward Greccio. Many came from far away, and the early winter darkness fell long before they could reach the town. The light of their torches might be seen on the open road, and the sound of their singing reached the gates of Greccio before them. That night the little town was almost as crowded as was Bethlehem on the eve of the first Christmas. The crowds were poor folk, for the most part, peasants from the fields, charcoal burners from the mountains, shepherds in their sheepskin coats and trousers, made with the wool outside, so that the wearers looked like strange, two-legged animals. The four shepherds who had slept so soundly a few nights before were of the company, but they knew nothing of their midnight visitors. The white dogs knew, but they could keep a secret. The shepherds were almost as quiet as their dogs. They always talked and sang less than other people, having grown used to long silences among their sheep.

Gathered at last into the square before the church, by the light of flaring torches, for the moon would rise late, the people saw with wonder and delight the surprise which Brother Francis and Sir John had prepared for them. They looked into a real stable. There was the manger full of hay, there were a live ox and a live ass. Even by torchlight their breath showed in the frosty air. And there, on the hay, lay a real baby, wrapped from the cold, asleep and smiling. It looked as sweet and innocent as the Christ Child Himself. The people shouted with delight. They clapped their hands and waved their torches.

Then there was silence, for Brother Francis stood before them, and the voice they loved so well, and had come so far to hear, began to read the old story of the birth of the Child Jesus, of the shepherds in the fields, and of the angels' song. When the reading was ended, Brother Francis talked to them as a father might speak to his children. He told of the love that is gentle as a little child, that is willing to be poor and humble as the Baby who was laid in a manger among the cattle. He begged his listeners to put anger and hatred and envy out of their hearts this Christmas Eve, and to think only thoughts of peace and good will. All listened eagerly while Brother Francis spoke, but the moment he finished the great crowd broke into singing. From the church tower the bells rang loud; the torches waved wildly, while voices here and there shouted for Brother Francis and for the Blessed Little Christ. Never before had such glorious hymns nor such joyous shouting been heard in the town of Greccio. Only the mothers, with babies in their arms, and the shepherds, in their woolly coats, looked on silently and thought: "We are in Bethlehem."

THE SIN OF THE PRINCE BISHOP

WILLIAM CANTON

The Prince Bishop Evrard stood gazing at his marvellous Cathedral; and as he let his eyes wander in delight over the three deep sculptured portals and the double gallery above them, and the great rose window, and the ringers' gallery, and so up to the massive western towers, he felt as though his heart were clapping hands for joy within him. And he thought to himself, "Surely in all the world God has no more beautiful house than this which I have built with such long labor and at so princely an outlay of my treasure." And thus the Prince Bishop fell into the sin of vainglory, and, though he was a holy man, he did not perceive that he had fallen, so filled with gladness was he at the sight of his completed work.

In the double gallery of the west front there were many great statues with crowns and sceptres, but a niche over the central portal was empty and this the Prince Bishop intended to fill with a statue of himself. It was to be a very small simple statue, as became one who prized lowliness of heart, but as he looked up at the vacant place it gave him pleasure to think that hundreds of years after he was dead people would pause before his effigy and praise him and his work. And this, too, was vainglory.

As the Prince Bishop lay asleep that night a mighty six-winged Angel stood beside him and bade him rise. "Come," he said, "and I will show thee some of those who have worked with thee in building the great church, and whose service in God's eyes has been more worthy than thine." And the Angel led him past the Cathedral and down the steep street of the ancient city, and though it was midday, the people going to and fro did not seem to see them. Beyond the gates they followed the shelving road till they came to green level fields, and there in the middle of the road, between grassy banks covered white with cherry blossom, two great white

113

oxen, yoked to a huge block of stone, stood resting before they began the toilsome ascent.

"Look!" said the Angel; and the Prince Bishop saw a little blue-winged bird which perched on the stout yoke beam fastened to the horns of the oxen, and sang such a heavenly song of rest and contentment that the big shaggy creatures ceased to blow stormily through their nostrils, and drew long tranquil breaths instead.

"Look again!" said the Angel. And from a hut of wattles and clay a little peasant girl came with a bundle of hay in her arms, and gave first one of the oxen and then the other a wisp. Then she stroked their black muzzles, and laid her rosy face against their white cheeks. Then the Prince Bishop saw the rude teamster rise from his rest on the bank and cry to his cattle, and the oxen strained against the beam and the thick ropes tightened, and the huge block of stone was once more set in motion.

And when the Prince Bishop saw that it was these fellow-workers whose service was more worthy in God's eyes than his own, he was abashed and sorrowful for his sin, and the tears of his own weeping awoke him. So he sent for the master of the sculptors and bade him fill the little niche over the middle portal, not with his own effigy but with an image of the child; and he bade him make two colossal figures of the white oxen; and to the great wonderment of the people these were set up high in the tower so that men could see them against the blue sky. "And as for me," he said, "let my body be buried, with my face downward, outside the great church, in front of the middle entrance, that men may trample on my vainglory and that I may serve them as a stepping-stone to the house of God; and the little child shall look on me when I lie in the dust."

Now the little girl in the niche was carved with wisps of hay in her hands, but the child who had fed the oxen knew nothing of this, and as she grew up she forgot her childish service, so that when she had grown to womanhood and chanced to see this statue over the portal she did not know it was her own self in stone. But what she had done was not forgotten in heaven.

And as for the oxen, one of them looked east and one looked west across the wide fruitful country about the foot of the hill-city. And one caught the first grey gleam, and the first rosy flush, and the first golden splendor of the sunrise; and the other was lit with the color of the sunset long after the lowlands had faded away in the blue mist of the twilight. Weary men and worn women looking up at them felt that a gladness and a glory and a deep peace had fallen on the life of toil. And then, when people began to understand, they said it was well that these mighty laborers, who had helped to build the house, should still find a place of service and honor in the house; and they remembered that the Master of the house had once been a Babe warmed in a manger by the breath of kine. And at the thought of this men grew more pitiful to their cattle, and to the beasts in servitude, and to all dumb animals. And that was one good fruit which sprang from the Prince Bishop's repentance.

Now over the colossal stone oxen hung the bells of the Cathedral. On Christmas Eve the ringers, according to the old custom, ascended to their gallery to ring in the birth of the Babe Divine. At the moment of midnight the master ringer gave the word, and the great bells began to swing in joyful sequence. Down below in the crowded church lay the image of the new-born Child on the cold straw, and at His haloed head stood the images of the ox and the ass. Far out across the snow-roofed city, far away over the white glistening country rang the glad music of the tower. People who went to their doors to listen cried in astonishment: "Hark! what strange music is that? It sounds as if the lowing of cattle were mingled with the chimes of the bells." In truth it was so. And in every byre the oxen and the kine answered the strange sweet cadences with their lowing, and the great stone oxen lowed back to their kin of the meadow through the deep notes of the joy-peal.

115

In the fulness of time the Prince Bishop Evrard died and was buried as he had willed, with his face humbly turned to the earth; and to this day the weather-wasted figure of the little girl looks down on him from her niche, and the slab over his grave serves as a stepping-stone to pious feet.

Taken by permission of E.P. Dutton and Company from "A Child's Book of Saints," by William Canton, Everyman's Library.

EARL SIGURD'S CHRISTMAS EVE

HJALMAR HJORTH BOYESEN

Earl Sigurd, he rides o'er the foam-crested brine,
  And he heeds not the billowy brawl,
For he yearns to behold gentle Swanwhite, the maid
  Who abides in Sir Burislav's hall.

"Earl Sigurd, the viking, he comes, he is near!
  Earl Sigurd, the scourge of the sea;
Among the wild rovers who dwell on the deep,
  There is none that is dreaded as he.

"Oh, hie ye, ye maidens, and hide where ye can,
  Ere the clang of his war-ax ye hear,
For the wolf of the woods has more pity than he,
  And his heart is as grim as his spear."

Thus rang the dread tidings, from castle to hut,
  Through the length of Sir Burislav's land,
As they spied the red pennon unfurled to the breeze,
  And the galleys that steered for the strand.

But with menacing brow, looming high in his prow
  Stood Earl Sigurd, and fair to behold
Was his bright, yellow hair, as it waved in the air,
  'Neath the glittering helmet of gold.

"Up, my comrades, and stand with your broadswords in hand,
  For the war is great Odin's delight;

And the Thunderer proud, how he laughs in his cloud
  When the Norsemen prepare for the fight!"

And the light galleys bore the fierce crew to the shore,
  And naught good did their coming forebode,
And a wail rose on high to the storm-riven sky
  As to Burislav's castle they strode.

Then the stout-hearted men of Sir Burislav's train
  To the gate-way came thronging full fast
And the battle-blade rang with a murderous clang,
  Borne aloft on the wings of the blast.

And they hewed and they thrust, till each man bit the dust,
  Their fierce valor availing them naught.
But the Thunderer proud, how he laughed in his cloud,
  When he saw how the Norsemen had fought!

Then came Burislav forth; to the men of the North
  Thus in quivering accents spake he:
"O, ye warriors, name me the ransom ye claim,
  Or in gold, or in robes, or in fee."

"Oh, what reck I thy gold?" quoth Earl Sigurd, the bold;
  "Has not Thor laid it all in my hand?
Give me Swanwhite, the fair, and by Balder I swear
  I shall never revisit thy land.

"For my vengeance speeds fast, and I come like the blast
  Of the night o'er the billowy brine;
I forget not thy scorn and thy laugh on that morn
  When I wooed me the maid that was mine."

Then the chief, sore afraid, brought the lily-white maid
  To the edge of the blood-sprinkled field,
And they bore her aloft o'er the sward of the croft
  On the vault of the glittering shield.

But amain in their path, in a whirlwind of wrath
  Came young Harold, Sir Burislav's son;
With a great voice he cried, while the echoes replied:
  "Lo, my vengeance, it cometh anon!"

Hark ye, Norsemen, hear great tidings:
  Odin, Thor, and Frey are dead,
And white Christ, the strong and gentle,
  standeth peace-crowned in their stead.

Lo, the blood-stained day of vengeance to the
  ancient night is hurled,
And the dawn of Christ is beaming blessings
  o'er the new-born world.

"See the Cross in splendor gleaming far and
  wide o'er pine-clad heath,
While the flaming blade of battle slumbers in
  its golden sheath.
And before the lowly Savior, e'en the rider of
  the sea,
Sigurd, tamer of the billow, he hath bent the
  stubborn knee."

Now at Yule-tide sat he feasting on the shore
  of Drontheim fiord,
And his stalwart swains about him watched
  the bidding of their lord.

Huge his strength was, but his visage, it was
  mild and fair to see;
Ne'er old Norway, heroes' mother, bore a
  mightier son than he.

With her maids sat gentle Swanwhite 'neath a
  roof of gleaming shields,
As the rarer lily blossoms 'mid the green herbs
  of the fields;

To and fro their merry words flew lightly
  through the torch-lit room,
Like a shuttle deftly skipping through the
  mazes of the loom.

And the scalds with nimble fingers o'er the
  sounding harp-strings swept;
Now the strain in laughter rippled, now with
  hidden woe it wept,
For they sang of Time's beginning, ere the sun
  the day brought forth—
Sang as sing the ocean breezes through the
  pine-woods of the North.

Bolder beat the breasts of Norsemen—when
  amid the tuneful din
Open sprang the heavy hall-doors, and a
  stranger entered in.
Tall his growth, though low he bended o'er a
  twisted staff of oak,
And his stalwart shape was folded in a dun,
  unseemly cloak.

Straight the Earl his voice uplifted: "Hail to thee, my guest austere! Drain with me this cup of welcome: thou shalt share our Yule-tide cheer. Thou shalt sit next to my high-seat e'en though lowly be thy birth, For to-night our Lord, the Savior, came a stranger to his earth."

Up then rose the gentle Swanwhite, and her
  eyes with fear grew bright;
Down the dusky hall she drifted, as a shadow
  drifts by night.
"If my lord would hold me worthy," low she
  spake, "then grant me leave
To abide between the stranger and my lord,
  this Christmas eve."

"Strange, O guest, is women's counsel, still
  their folly is the staff
Upon which our wisdom leaneth," and he
  laughed a burly laugh;
Lifted up her lissome body with a husband's
  tender pride,
Kissed her brow, and placed her gently in the
  high-seat at his side.

But the guest stood pale and quivered, where
  the red flames roofward rose,
And he clenched the brimming goblet in his
  fingers, fierce and close,

Then he spake: "All hail, Earl Sigurd,
  mightiest of the Norsemen, hail!
Ere I name to thee my tidings, I will taste thy
  flesh and ale."

Quoth the merry Earl with fervor: "Courteous
   is thy speech and free:
While thy worn soul thou refreshest, I will
   sing a song to thee;
For beneath that dusky garment thou mayst
   hide a hero's heart,
And my hand, though stiff, hath scarcely yet
   unlearned the singer's art."

Then the arms so tightly folded round his neck
   the Earl unclasped,
And his heart was stirred within him as the
   silvern strings he grasped,
But with eyes of meek entreaty, closely to his
   side she clung,
While his mighty soul rose upward on the
   billows of the song.

For he sang, in tones impassioned, of the death
   of Aesir bright,
Sang the song of Christ the glorious, who was
   born a babe to-night,

How the hosts of heaven victorious joined the
   anthem of his birth,
Of the kings the starlight guided from the far
   lands of the earth.

And anon, with bodeful glamour fraught, the
   hurrying strain sped on,
As he sang the law of vengeance and the wrath
   forever gone,
Sang of gods with murder sated, who had laid

the fair earth waste,
Who had whetted swords of Norsemen,
  plunged them into Norsemen's breast.

But he shook a shower of music, rippling from
  the silver strings,
And bright visions rose of angels and of fair
  and shining things
As he sang of heaven's rejoicing at the mild
  and bloodless reign
Of the gentle Christ who bringeth peace and
  good-will unto men!

But the guest sat dumb and hearkened, staring
  at the brimming bowl,
While the lay with mighty wing-beats swept
  the darkness of his soul.

For the Christ who worketh wonders as of old,
  so e'en to-day
Sent his angel downward gliding on the ladder
  of the lay.

As the host his song had ended with a last
  resounding twang,
And within the harp's dumb chambers
  murmurous echoes faintly rang,
Up then sprang the guest, and straightway
  downward rolled his garment dun—
There stood Harold, the avenger, Burislav's
  undaunted son.

High he loomed above the feasters in the
  torchlight dim and weird,
From his eyes hot tears were streaming,
  sparkling in his tawny beard;
Shining in his sea-blue mantle stood he, 'mid
  that wondering throng,
And each maiden thought him fairest, and each
  warrior vowed him strong.

Swift he bared his blade of battle, flung it
  quivering on the board:
"Lo!" he cried, "I came to bid thee baleful
  greeting with my sword;
Thou hast dulled the edge that never shrank
  from battle's fiercest test—
Now I come, as comes a brother, swordless unto
  brother's breast.

"With three hundred men I landed in the
  gloaming at thy shore—
Dost thou hear their axes clanking on their
  shields without thy door?
But a yearning woke within me my sweet sister's
  voice to hear,
To behold her face and whisper words of
  warning in her ear.

"But I knew not of the new-born king, who
  holds the earth in sway,
And whose voice like fragrance blended in the
  soarings of thy lay.
This my vengeance now, O brother: foes as
  friends shall hands unite;

Teach me, thou, the wondrous tidings, and the
law of Christ the white."

Touched as by an angel's glory, strangely
shone Earl Sigurd's face,
As he locked his foe, his brother, in a brotherly
embrace;

And each warrior upward leaping, swung his
horn with gold bedight:
"Hail to Sigurd, hail to Harold, three times
hail to Christ the white!"

A CHRISTMAS LEGEND

FLORENCE SCANNELL

It was Christmas Eve. The night was very dark and the snow falling fast, as Hermann, the charcoal-burner, drew his cloak tighter around him, and the wind whistled fiercely through the trees of the Black Forest. He had been to carry a load to a castle near, and was now hastening home to his little hut. Although he worked very hard, he was poor, gaining barely enough for the wants of his wife and his four little children. He was thinking of them, when he heard a faint wailing. Guided by the sound, he groped about and found a little child, scantily clothed, shivering and sobbing by itself in the snow.

"Why, little one, have they left thee here all alone to face this cruel blast?"

The child answered nothing, but looked piteously up in the charcoal-burner's face.

"Well, I cannot leave thee here. Thou would'st be dead before the morning."

So saying, Hermann raised it in his arms, wrapping it in his cloak and warming its little cold hands in his bosom. When he arrived at his hut, he put down the child and tapped at the door, which was immediately thrown open, and the children rushed to meet him.

"Here, wife, is a guest to our Christmas Eve supper," said he, leading in the little one, who held timidly to his finger with its tiny hand.

"And welcome he is," said the wife. "Now let him come and warm himself by the fire."

The children all pressed round to welcome and gaze at the little new-comer. They showed him their pretty fir-tree, decorated with bright, colored lamps in honor of Christmas Eve, which the good mother had endeavored to make a *fête* for the children.

Then they sat down to supper, each child contributing of its portion for the guest, looking with admiration at its clear, blue eyes and golden hair, which shone so as to shed a brighter light in the little room; and as they gazed, it grew into a sort of halo round his head, and his eyes beamed with a heavenly luster. Soon two white wings appeared at his shoulders, and he seemed to grow larger and larger, and then the beautiful vision vanished, spreading out his hands as in benediction over them.

Hermann and his wife fell on their knees, exclaiming, in awe-struck voices: "The holy Christ-child!" and then embraced their wondering children in joy and thankfulness that they had entertained the Heavenly Guest.

The next morning, as Hermann passed by the place where he had found the fair child, he saw a cluster of lovely white flowers, with dark green leaves, looking as though the snow itself had blossomed. Hermann plucked some, and carried them reverently home to his wife and children, who treasured the fair blossoms and tended them carefully in remembrance of that wonderful Christmas Eve, calling them Chrysanthemums; and every year, as the time came round, they put aside a portion of their feast and gave it to some poor little child, according to the words of the Christ: "Inasmuch as ye have done it unto one of the least of these my brethren, ye have done it unto me."

THE LEGEND OF THE CHRISTMAS ROSE

SELMA LAGERLÖF

Robber Mother, who lived in Robbers' Cave up in Göinge forest, went down to the village one day on a begging tour. Robber Father, who was an outlawed man, did not dare to leave the forest, but had to content himself with lying in wait for the wayfarers who ventured within its borders. But at that time travellers were not very plentiful in Southern Skåne. If it so happened that the man had had a few weeks of ill luck with his hunt, his wife would take to the road. She took with her five youngsters, and each youngster wore a ragged leathern suit and birch-bark shoes and bore a sack on his back as long as himself. When Robber Mother stepped inside the door of a cabin, no one dared refuse to give her whatever she demanded; for she was not above coming back the following night and setting fire to the house if she had not been well received. Robber Mother and her brood were worse than a pack of wolves, and many a man felt like running a spear through them; but it was never done, because they all knew that the man stayed up in the forest, and he would have known how to wreak vengeance if anything had happened to the children or the old woman.

Now that Robber Mother went from house to house and begged, she came one day to Övid, which at that time was a cloister. She rang the bell of the cloister gate and asked for food. The watchman let down a small wicket in the gate and handed her six round bread cakes—one for herself and one for each of the five children.

While the mother was standing quietly at the gate, her youngsters were running about. And now one of them came and pulled at her skirt, as a signal that he had discovered something which she ought to come and see, and Robber Mother followed him promptly.

The entire cloister was surrounded by a high and strong wall, but the youngster had managed to find a little back gate which stood ajar. When Robber Mother got there, she pushed the gate open and walked inside without asking leave, as it was her custom to do.

Övid Cloister was managed at that time by Abbot Hans, who knew all about herbs. Just within the cloister wall he had planted a little herb garden, and it was into this that the old woman had forced her way.

At first glance Robber Mother was so astonished that she paused at the gate. It was high summertide, and Abbot Hans' garden was so full of flowers that the eyes were fairly dazzled by the blues, reds, and yellows, as one looked into it. But presently an indulgent smile spread over her features, and she started to walk up a narrow path that lay between many flower-beds.

In the garden a lay brother walked about, pulling up weeds. It was he who had left the door in the wall open, that he might throw the weeds and tares on the rubbish heap outside.

When he saw Robber Mother coming in, with all five youngsters in tow, he ran toward her at once and ordered them away. But the beggar woman walked right on as before. She cast her eyes up and down, looking now at the stiff white lilies which spread near the ground, then on the ivy climbing high upon the cloister wall, and took no notice whatever of the lay brother.

He thought she had not understood him, and wanted to take her by the arm and turn her toward the gate. But when the robber woman saw his purpose, she gave him a look that sent him reeling backward. She had been walking with back bent under her beggar's pack, but now she straightened herself to her full height. "I am Robber Mother from Göinge forest; so touch me if you dare!" And it was obvious that she was as certain she would be left in peace as if she had announced that she was the Queen of Denmark.

And yet the lay brother dared to oppose her, although now, when he knew who she was, he spoke reasonably to her. "You must know, Robber Mother, that this is a monks' cloister, and no woman in the land is allowed within these walls. If you do not go away, the monks will be angry with me because I forgot to close the gate, and perhaps they will drive me away from the cloister and the herb garden."

But such prayers were wasted on Robber Mother. She walked straight ahead among the little flower-beds and looked at the hyssop with its magenta blossoms, and at the honeysuckles, which were full of deep orange-colored flower clusters.

Then the lay brother knew of no other remedy than to run into the cloister and call for help.

He returned with two stalwart monks, and Robber Mother saw that now it meant business! With feet firmly planted she stood in the path and began shrieking in strident tones all the awful vengeance she would wreak on the cloister if she couldn't remain in the herb garden as long as she wished. But the monks did not see why they need fear her and thought only of driving her out. Then Robber Mother let out a perfect volley of shrieks, and, throwing herself upon the monks, clawed and bit at them; so did all the youngsters. The men soon learned that she could overpower them, and all they could do was to go back into the cloister for reinforcements.

As they ran through the passage-way which led to the cloister, they met Abbot Hans, who came rushing out to learn what all this noise was about.

Then they had to confess that Robber Mother from Göinge forest had come into the cloister and that they were unable to drive her out and must call for assistance.

But Abbot Hans upbraided them for using force and forbade their calling for help. He sent both monks back to their work, and although he was an old and fragile man, he took with him only the lay brother.

When Abbot Hans came out in the garden, Robber Mother was still wandering among the flower-beds. He regarded her with astonishment. He was certain that Robber Mother had never before seen an herb garden; yet she sauntered leisurely between all the small patches, each of which had been planted with its own species of rare flower, and looked at them as if they were old acquaintances. At some she smiled, at others she shook her head.

Abbot Hans loved his herb garden as much as it was possible for him to love anything earthly and perishable. Wild and terrible as the old woman looked, he couldn't help liking that she had fought with three monks for the privilege of viewing the garden in peace. He came up to her and asked in a mild tone if the garden pleased her.

Robber Mother turned defiantly toward Abbot Hans, for she expected only to be trapped and overpowered. But when she noticed his white hair and bent form, she answered peaceably, "First, when I saw this, I thought I had never seen a prettier garden; but now I see that it can't be compared with one I know of."

Abbot Hans had certainly expected a different answer. When he heard that Robber Mother had seen a garden more beautiful than his, a faint flush spread over his withered cheek. The lay brother, who was standing close by, immediately began to censure the old woman. "This is Abbot Hans," said he, "who with much care and diligence has gathered the flowers from far and near for his herb garden. We all know that there is not a more beautiful garden to be found in all Skåne, and it is not befitting that you, who live in the wild forest all the year around, should find fault with his work."

"I don't wish to make myself the judge of either him or you," said Robber Mother. "I'm only saying that if you could see the garden of which I am thinking you would uproot all the flowers planted here and cast them away like weeds."

But the Abbot's assistant was hardly less proud of the flowers than the Abbot himself, and after hearing her remarks he laughed derisively. "I can understand that you only talk like this to tease us. It must be a pretty garden that you have made for yourself amongst the pines in Göinge forest! I'd be willing to wager my soul's salvation that you have never before been within the walls of an herb garden."

Robber Mother grew crimson with rage to think that her word was doubted, and she cried out: "It may be true that until to-day I had never been within the walls of an herb garden; but you monks, who are holy men, certainly must know that on every Christmas Eve the great Göinge forest is transformed into a beautiful garden, to commemorate the hour of our Lord's birth. We who live in the forest have seen this happen every year. And in that garden I have seen flowers so lovely that I dared not lift my hand to pluck them."

The lay brother wanted to continue the argument, but Abbot Hans gave him a sign to be silent. For, ever since his childhood, Abbot Hans had heard it said that on every Christmas Eve the forest was dressed in holiday glory. He had often longed to see it, but he had never had the good fortune. Eagerly he begged and implored Robber Mother that he might come up to the Robbers' Cave on Christmas Eve. If she would only send one of her children to show him the way, he could ride up there alone, and he would never betray them—on the contrary, he would reward them, in so far as it lay in his power.

Robber Mother said no at first, for she was thinking of Robber Father and of the peril which might befall him should she permit Abbot Hans to ride up to their cave. At the same time the desire to prove to the monk that the garden which she knew was more beautiful than his got the better of her, and she gave in.

"But more than one follower you cannot take with you," said she, "and you are not to waylay us or trap us, as sure as you are a holy man."

This Abbot Hans promised, and then Robber Mother went her way. Abbot Hans commanded the lay brother not to reveal to a soul that which had been agreed upon. He feared that the monks, should they learn of his purpose, would not allow a man of his years to go up to the Robbers' Cave.

Nor did he himself intend to reveal his project to a human being. And then it happened that Archbishop Absalon from Lund came to Övid and remained through the night. When Abbot Hans was showing him the herb garden, he got to thinking of Robber Mother's visit, and the lay brother, who was at work in the garden, heard Abbot Hans telling the Bishop about Robber Father, who these many years had lived as an outlaw in the forest, and asking him for a letter of ransom for the man, that he might lead an honest life among respectable folk. "As things are now," said Abbot Hans, "his children are growing up into worse malefactors than himself, and you will soon have a whole gang of robbers to deal with up there in the forest."

But the Archbishop replied that he did not care to let the robber loose among honest folk in the villages. It would be best for all that he remain in the forest.

Then Abbot Hans grew zealous and told the Bishop all about Göinge forest, which, every year at Yuletide, clothed itself in summer bloom around the Robbers' Cave. "If these bandits are not so bad but that God's glories can be made manifest to them, surely we cannot be too wicked to experience the same blessing."

The Archbishop knew how to answer Abbot Hans. "This much I will promise you, Abbot Hans," he said, smiling, "that any day you send me a blossom from the garden in Göinge forest, I will give you letters of ransom for all the outlaws you may choose to plead for."

The lay brother apprehended that Bishop Absalon believed as little in this story of Robber Mother's as he himself; but Abbot Hans perceived nothing of the sort, but thanked Absalon for his good promise and said that he would surely send him the flower.

Abbot Hans had his way. And the following Christmas Eve he did not sit at home with his monks in Övid Cloister, but was on his way to Göinge forest. One of Robber Mother's wild youngsters ran ahead of him, and close behind him was the lay brother who had talked with Robber Mother in the herb garden.

Abbot Hans had been longing to make this journey, and he was very happy now that it had come to pass. But it was a different matter with the lay brother who accompanied him. Abbot Hans was very dear to him, and he would not willingly have allowed another to attend him and watch over him; but he didn't believe that he should see any Christmas Eve garden. He thought the whole thing a snare which Robber Mother had, with great cunning, laid for Abbot Hans, that he might fall into her husband's clutches.

While Abbot Hans was riding toward the forest, he saw that everywhere they were preparing to celebrate Christmas. In every peasant settlement fires were lighted in the bathhouse to warm it for the afternoon bathing. Great hunks of meat and bread were being carried from the larders into the cabins, and from the barns came the men with big sheaves of straw to be strewn over the floors.

As he rode by the little country churches, he observed that each parson, with his sexton, was busily engaged in decorating his church; and when he came to the road which leads to Bösjo Cloister, he observed that all the poor of the parish were coming with armfuls of bread and long candles, which they had received at the cloister gate.

When Abbot Hans saw all these Christmas preparations, his haste increased. He was thinking of the festivities that awaited him, which were greater than any the others would be privileged to enjoy.

But the lay brother whined and fretted when he saw how they were preparing to celebrate Christmas in every humble cottage. He grew more and more anxious, and begged and implored Abbot Hans to turn back and not to throw himself deliberately into the robber's hands.

Abbot Hans went straight ahead, paying no heed to his lamentations. He left the plain behind him and came up into desolate and wild forest regions. Here the road was bad, almost like a stony and burr-strewn path, with neither bridge nor plank to help them over brooklet and rivulet. The farther they rode, the colder it grew, and after a while they came upon snow-covered ground.

It turned out to be a long and hazardous ride through the forest. They climbed steep and slippery side paths, crawled over swamp and marsh, and pushed through windfall and bramble. Just as daylight was waning, the robber boy guided them across a forest meadow, skirted by tall, naked leaf trees and green fir trees. Back of the meadow loomed a mountain wall, and in this wall they saw a door of thick boards. Now

Abbot Hans understood that they had arrived, and dismounted. The child opened the heavy door for him, and he looked into a poor mountain grotto, with bare stone walls. Robber Mother was seated before a log fire that burned in the middle of the floor. Alongside the walls were beds of virgin pine and moss, and on one of these beds lay Robber Father asleep.

"Come in, you out there!" shouted Robber Mother without rising, "and fetch the horses in with you, so they won't be destroyed by the night cold."

Abbot Hans walked boldly into the cave, and the lay brother followed. Here were wretchedness and poverty! and nothing was done to celebrate Christmas. Robber Mother had neither brewed nor baked; she had neither washed nor scoured. The youngsters were lying on the floor around a kettle, eating; but no better food was provided for them than a watery gruel.

Robber Mother spoke in a tone as haughty and dictatorial as any well-to-do peasant woman. "Sit down by the fire and warm yourself, Abbot Hans," said she; "and if you have food with you, eat, for the food which we in the forest prepare you wouldn't care to taste. And if you are tired after the long journey, you can lie down on one of these beds to sleep. You needn't be afraid of oversleeping, for I'm sitting here by the fire keeping watch. I shall awaken you in time to see that which you have come up here to see."

Abbot Hans obeyed Robber Mother and brought forth his food sack; but he was so fatigued after the journey he was hardly able to eat, and as soon as he could stretch himself on the bed, he fell asleep.

The lay brother was also assigned a bed to rest upon, but he didn't dare sleep, as he thought he had better keep his eye on Robber Father to prevent his getting up and capturing Abbot Hans. But gradually fatigue got the better of him, too, and he dropped into a doze.

When he woke up, he saw that Abbot Hans had left his bed and was sitting by the fire talking with Robber Mother. The outlawed robber sat also by the fire. He was a tall, raw-boned man with a dull, sluggish appearance. His back was turned to Abbot Hans, as though he would have it appear that he was not listening to the conversation.

Abbot Hans was telling Robber Mother all about the Christmas preparations he had seen on the journey, reminding her of Christmas feasts and games which she must have known in her youth, when she lived at peace with mankind. "I'm sorry for your children, who can never run on the village street in holiday dress or tumble in the Christmas straw," said he.

At first Robber Mother answered in short, gruff sentences, but by degrees she became more subdued and listened more intently. Suddenly Robber Father turned toward Abbot Hans and shook his clenched fist in his face. "You miserable monk! did you come here to coax from me my wife and children? Don't you know that I am an outlaw and may not leave the forest?"

Abbot Hans looked him fearlessly in the eyes. "It is my purpose to get a letter of ransom for you from Archbishop Absalon," said he. He had hardly finished speaking when the robber and his wife burst out laughing. They knew well enough the kind of mercy a forest robber could expect from Bishop Absalon!

"Oh, if I get a letter of ransom from Absalon," said Robber Father, "then I'll promise you that never again will I steal so much as a goose."

The lay brother was annoyed with the robber folk for daring to laugh at Abbot Hans, but on his own account he was well pleased. He had seldom seen the Abbot sitting more peaceful and meek with his monks at Övid than he now sat with this wild robber folk.

Suddenly Robber Mother rose. "You sit here and talk, Abbot Hans," she said, "so that we are forgetting to look at the forest. Now I can hear, even in this cave, how the Christmas bells are ringing."

The words were barely uttered when they all sprang up and rushed out. But in the forest it was still dark night and bleak winter. The only thing they marked was a distant clang borne on a light south wind.

"How can this bell ringing ever awaken the dead forest?" thought Abbot Hans. For now, as he stood out in the winter darkness, he thought it far more impossible that a summer garden could spring up here than it had seemed to him before.

When the bells had been ringing a few moments, a sudden illumination penetrated the forest; the next moment it was dark again, and then the light came back. It pushed its way forward between the stark trees, like a shimmering mist. This much it effected: The darkness merged into a faint daybreak. Then Abbot Hans saw that the snow had vanished from the ground, as if some one had removed a carpet, and the earth began to take on a green covering. Then the ferns shot up their fronds, rolled like a bishop's staff. The heather that grew on the stony hills and the bog-myrtle rooted in the ground moss dressed themselves quickly in new bloom. The moss-tufts thickened and raised themselves, and the spring blossoms shot upward their swelling buds, which already had a touch of color.

Abbot Hans' heart beat fast as he marked the first signs of the forest's awakening. "Old man that I am, shall I behold such a miracle?" thought he, and the tears wanted to spring to his eyes. Again it grew so hazy that he feared the darkness would once more cover the earth; but almost immediately there came a new wave of light. It brought with it the splash of rivulet and the rush of cataract. Then the leaves of the trees burst into bloom, as if a swarm of green butterflies came flying and clustered on the branches. It was not only trees and plants that awoke, but crossbeaks hopped from branch to branch, and the woodpeckers hammered on the limbs until the splinters fairly flew around them. A flock of starlings from up country lighted in a fir top to rest. They were paradise starlings. The tips of each tiny feather shone in brilliant reds, and, as the birds moved, they glittered like so many jewels.

Again, all was dark for an instant, but soon there came a new light wave. A fresh, warm south wind blew and scattered over the forest meadow all the little seeds that had been brought here from southern lands by birds and ships and winds, and which could not thrive elsewhere because of this country's cruel cold. These took root and sprang up the instant they touched the ground.

When the next warm wind came along, the blueberries and lignon ripened. Cranes and wild geese shrieked in the air, the bullfinches built nests, and the baby squirrels began playing on the branches of the trees.

Everything came so fast now that Abbot Hans could not stop to reflect on how immeasurably great was the miracle that was taking place. He had time only to use his eyes and ears. The next light wave that came rushing in brought with it the scent of newly ploughed acres, and far off in the distance the milkmaids were heard coaxing the cows—and the tinkle of the sheep's bells. Pine and spruce trees were so thickly clothed with red cones that they shone like crimson mantles. The juniper berries changed color every second, and forest flowers covered the ground till it was all red, blue, and yellow.

Abbot Hans bent down to the earth and broke off a wild strawberry blossom, and, as he straightened up, the berry ripened in his hand.

The mother fox came out of her lair with a big litter of black-legged young. She went up to Robber Mother and scratched at her skirt, and

Robber Mother bent down to her and praised her young. The horned owl, who had just begun his night chase, was astonished at the light and went back to his ravine to perch for the night. The male cuckoo crowed, and his mate stole up to the nests of the little birds with her egg in her mouth.

Robber Mother's youngsters let out perfect shrieks of delight. They stuffed themselves with wild strawberries that hung on the bushes, large as pine cones. One of them played with a litter of young hares; another ran a race with some young crows, which had hopped from their nest before they were really ready; a third caught up an adder from the ground and wound it around his neck and arm.

Robber Father was standing out on a marsh eating raspberries. When he glanced up, a big black bear stood beside him. Robber Father broke off an osier twig and struck the bear on the nose. "Keep to your own ground, you!" he said; "this is my turf." Then the huge bear turned around and lumbered off in another direction.

New waves of warmth and light kept coming, and now they brought with them seeds from the star-flower. Golden pollen from rye fields fairly flew in the air. Then came butterflies, so big that they looked like flying lilies. The bee-hive in a hollow oak was already so full of honey that it dripped down on the trunk of the tree. Then all the flowers whose seeds had been brought from foreign lands began to blossom. The loveliest roses climbed up the mountain wall in a race with the blackberry vines, and from the forest meadow sprang flowers as large as human faces.

Abbot Hans thought of the flower he was to pluck for Bishop Absalon; but each new flower that appeared was more beautiful than the others, and he wanted to choose the most beautiful of all.

Wave upon wave kept coming until the air was so filled with light that it glittered. All the life and beauty and joy of summer smiled on Abbot

Hans. He felt that earth could bring no greater happiness than that which welled up about him, and he said to himself, "I do not know what new beauties the next wave that comes can bring with it."

But the light kept streaming in, and now it seemed to Abbot Hans that it carried with it something from an infinite distance. He felt a celestial atmosphere enfolding him, and tremblingly he began to anticipate, now that earth's joys had come, the glories of heaven were approaching.

Then Abbot Hans marked how all grew still; the birds hushed their songs, the flowers ceased growing, and the young foxes played no more. The glory now nearing was such that the heart wanted to stop beating; the eyes wept without one's knowing it; the soul longed to soar away into the Eternal. From far in the distance faint harp tones were heard, and celestial song, like a soft murmur, reached him.

Abbot Hans clasped his hands and dropped to his knees. His face was radiant with bliss. Never had he dreamed that even in this life it should be granted him to taste the joys of heaven, and to hear angels sing Christmas carols!

But beside Abbot Hans stood the lay brother who had accompanied him. In his mind there were dark thoughts. "This cannot be a true miracle," he thought, "since it is revealed to malefactors. This does not come from God, but has its origin in witchcraft and is sent hither by Satan. It is the Evil One's power that is tempting us and compelling us to see that which has no real existence."

From afar were heard the sound of angel harps and the tones of a Miserere.
But the lay brother thought it was the evil spirits of hell coming closer. "They would enchant and seduce us," sighed he, "and we shall be sold into perdition."

The angel throng was so near now that Abbot Hans saw their bright forms through the forest branches. The lay brother saw them, too; but back of all this wondrous beauty he saw only some dread evil. For him it was the devil who performed these wonders on the anniversary of our Saviour's birth. It was done simply for the purpose of more effectually deluding poor human beings.

All the while the birds had been circling around the head of Abbot Hans, and they let him take them in his hands. But all the animals were afraid of the lay brother; no bird perched on his shoulder, no snake played at his feet. Then there came a little forest dove. When she marked that the angels were nearing, she plucked up courage and flew down on the lay brother's shoulder and laid her head against his cheek.

Then it appeared to him as if sorcery were come right upon him, to tempt and corrupt him. He struck with his hand at the forest dove and cried in such a loud voice that it rang throughout the forest, "Go thou back to hell, whence thou art come!"

Just then the angels were so near that Abbot Hans felt the feathery touch of their great wings, and he bowed down to earth in reverent greeting.

But when the lay brother's words sounded, their song was hushed and the holy guests turned in flight. At the same time the light and the mild warmth vanished in unspeakable terror for the darkness and cold in a human heart. Darkness sank over the earth, like a coverlet; frost came, all the growths shrivelled up; the animals and birds hastened away; the rushing of streams was hushed; the leaves dropped from the trees, rustling like rain.

Abbot Hans felt how his heart, which had but lately swelled with bliss, was now contracting with insufferable agony. "I can never outlive this," thought he, "that the angels from heaven had been so close to me and were driven away; that they wanted to sing Christmas carols for me and were driven to flight."

Then he remembered the flower he had promised Bishop Absalon, and at the last moment he fumbled among the leaves and moss to try and find a blossom. But he sensed how the ground under his fingers froze and how the white snow came gliding over the ground. Then his heart caused him ever greater anguish. He could not rise, but fell prostrate on the ground and lay there.

When the robber folk and the lay brother had groped their way back to the cave, they missed Abbot Hans. They took brands with them and went out to search for him. They found him dead upon the coverlet of snow.

Then the lay brother began weeping and lamenting, for he understood that it was he who had killed Abbot Hans because he had dashed from him the cup of happiness which he had been thirsting to drain to its last drop.

When Abbot Hans had been carried down to Övid, those who took charge of the dead saw that he held his right hand locked tight around something which he must have grasped at the moment of death. When they finally got his hand open, they found that the thing which he had held in such an iron grip was a pair of white root bulbs, which he had torn from among the moss and leaves.

When the lay brother who had accompanied Abbot Hans saw the bulbs, he took them and planted them in Abbot Hans' herb garden.

He guarded them the whole year to see if any flower would spring from them. But in vain he waited through the spring, the summer, and the autumn. Finally, when winter had set in and all the leaves, and the flowers were dead, he ceased caring for them.

But when Christmas Eve came again, he was so strongly reminded of Abbot Hans that he wandered out into the garden to think of him. And look! as he came to the spot where he had planted the bare root bulbs, he saw that from them had sprung flourishing green stalks, which bore beautiful flowers with silver white leaves.

He called out all the monks at Övid, and when they saw that this plant bloomed on Christmas Eve, when all the other growths were as if dead, they understood that this flower had in truth been plucked by Abbot Hans from the Christmas garden in Göinge forest. Then the lay brother asked the monks if he might take a few blossoms to Bishop Absalon.

And when he appeared before Bishop Absalon, he gave him the flowers and said: "Abbot Hans sends you these. They are the flowers he promised to pick for you from the garden in Göinge forest."

When Bishop Absalon beheld the flowers, which had sprung from the earth in darkest winter, and heard the words, he turned as pale as if he had met a ghost. He sat in silence a moment; thereupon he said, "Abbot Hans has faithfully kept his word and I shall also keep mine." And he ordered that a letter of ransom be drawn up for the wild robber who was outlawed and had been forced to live in the forest ever since his youth.

He handed the letter to the lay brother, who departed at once for the Robbers' Cave. When he stepped in there on Christmas Day, the robber came toward him with axe uplifted. "I'd like to hack you monks into bits, as many as you are!" said he. "It must be your fault that Göinge forest did not last night dress itself in Christmas bloom."

"The fault is mine alone," said the lay brother, "and I will gladly die for it; but first I must deliver a message from Abbot Hans." And he drew forth the Bishop's letter and told the man that he was free. "Hereafter you and your children shall play in the Christmas straw and celebrate your Christmas among people, just as Abbot Hans wished to have it," said he.

Then Robber Father stood there pale and speechless, but Robber Mother said in his name, "Abbot Hans has indeed kept his word, and Robber Father will keep his."

When the robber and his wife left the cave, the lay brother moved in and lived all alone in the forest, in constant meditation and prayer that his hard-heartedness might be forgiven him.

But Göinge forest never again celebrated the hour of our Saviour's birth; and of all its glory, there lives to-day only the plant which Abbot Hans had plucked. It has been named CHRISTMAS ROSE. And each year at Christmastide she sends forth from the earth her green stalks and white blossoms, as if she never could forget that she had once grown in the great Christmas garden at Göinge forest.

FÉLIX

By EVALEEN STEIN

A very long while ago, perhaps as many as two hundred years, the little Provençal village of Sur Varne was all bustle and stir, for it was the week before Christmas; and always, in all the world, no one has known better how to keep the joyous holiday than have the happy-hearted people of Provence, the southeastern corner of France.

Everybody was busy, hurrying to and fro, gathering garlands of myrtle and laurel, bringing home their Yule logs with pretty old songs and ceremonies, and in various ways making ready for the all-important festival.

Not a house in Sur Varne but in some manner told the coming of the blessed birthday, and especially were there great preparations in the cottage of the shepherd, Père Michaud. This cottage, covered with white stucco, and thatched with long marsh-grass, stood at the edge of the village; olive and mulberry trees clustered about it, and a wild jasmine vine clambered over the doorway, while on this particular morning all around the low projecting eaves hung a row of tiny wheat-sheaves, swinging in the crisp December air, and twinkling in the sunlight like a golden fringe. For the Père Michaud had been up betimes, making ready the Christmas feast for the birds, which no Provençal peasant ever forgets at this gracious season; and the birds knew it, for already dozens of saucy robins and linnets and fieldfares were gathering in the Père's mulberry-trees, their mouths fairly watering with anticipation.

Within the cottage the good dame, the Misè Michaud, with wide sleeves rolled up and kirtle tucked back, was hard at work making all manner of savory goodies, while in the huge oven beside the blazing hearth the great Christmas cakes were baking, the famous *pompou* and *fougasse*, as they were called, dear to the hearts of the children of old Provence.

Now and then, as the cottage door swung open on the dame's various cookery errands, one might hear a faint "Baa, baa!" from the sheepfold, where little Félix Michaud was very busy also.

Through the crevices of its weather-beaten boards came the sound of vigorous scrubbing of wool, and sometimes an impatient "Ninette! Ninette!—thou silly sheep! Wilt thou never stand still?" Or else, in a softer tone, an eager "Beppo, my little Beppo, dost thou know? Dost thou know?" To all of which there would come no answer save the lamb's weak little "Baa, baa!"

For Ninette, Beppo's mother, was a silly old sheep, and Beppo was a very young little lamb, and so they could not possibly be expected to know what a great honor had suddenly befallen them. They did not dream that, the night before, Père Michaud had told Félix that his Beppo (for Beppo was Félix's very own) had been chosen by the shepherds for the "offered lamb" of the Christmas Eve procession in all its festival splendor in the great church of the village.

Of the importance of this procession in the eyes of the peasant folk I will tell you more by and by; it is enough to say now that to be the offered lamb, or indeed the offered lamb's mother, for both always went together, was the greatest honor and glory that could possibly happen to a Provençal sheep, and so little Félix was fairly bursting with pride and delight. And so it was, too, that he was now busying himself washing their wool, which he determined should shine like spun silver on the great night.

He tugged away, scrubbing and brushing and combing the thick fleeces, and at last, after much labor, considered their toilets done for the day;

then, giving each a handful of fresh hay to nibble, he left the fold and trudged into the cottage.

"Well, little one," said the Misè, "hast thou finished thy work?"

"Yes, mother," answered Félix; "and I shall scrub them so each day till the holy night! Even now Ninette is white as milk, and Beppo shines like an angel! Ah, but I shall be proud when he rides up to the altar in his little cart! And, mother, dost thou not really think him far handsomer than was Jean's lamb, that stupid Nano, in the procession last year?"

"There, there," said the Misè, "never thou mind about Jean's lamb, but run along now and finish thy crèche."

Now, in Provence, at the time when Félix lived, no one had ever heard of such a thing as a Christmas tree; but in its stead every cottage had a "crèche"; that is, in one corner of the great living-room, the room of the fireplace, the peasant children and their fathers and mothers built up on a table a mimic village of Bethlehem, with houses and people and animals, and, above all, with the manger, where the Christ Child lay. Everyone took the greatest pains to make the crèche as perfect as possible, and some even went so far as to fasten tiny angels to the rafters, so that they hovered over the toy houses like a flock of white butterflies; and sometimes a gold star, hung on a golden thread, quivered over the little manger, in memory of the wonderful star of the Magi.

In the Michaud cottage the crèche was already well under way. In the corner across from the fireplace the Père had built up a mound, and this Félix had covered with bits of rock and tufts of grass, and little green boughs for trees, all to represent the rocky hillside of Judea; then, half-way up, he began to place the tiny houses. These he had cut out of wood and adorned with wonderful carving, in which, indeed, he was very skilful. And then, such figures as he had made, such quaint little men and women, such marvelous animals, camels and oxen and sheep and horses, were never before seen in Sur Varne. But the figure on which he had lavished his utmost skill was that of the little Christ Child, which was not to be placed in the manger until Christmas night itself.

Félix kept this figure in his blouse pocket, carefully wrapped up in a bit of wool, and he spent all his spare moments striving to give it some fresh beauty; for I will tell you a secret: poor little Félix had a great passion for carving, and the one thing for which he longed above all others was to be allowed to apprentice himself in the workshop of Père Videau, who was the master carver of the village, and whose beautiful work on the portals of the great church was the admiration of Félix's heart. He longed, too, for better tools than the rude little knife he had, and for days and years in which to learn to use them.

But the Père Michaud had scant patience with these notions of the little son's, and once, when Félix had ventured to speak to him about it, had insisted rather sharply that he was to stick to his sheep-tending, so that when the Père himself grew old he could take charge of the flocks and keep the family in bread; for the Père had small faith in the art of the carver as being able to supply the big brown loaves that the Misè baked every week in the great stone oven. So Félix was obliged to go on minding the flocks; but whenever he had a moment of his own, he employed it in carving a bit of wood or chipping at a fragment of soft stone.

But while I have stopped to tell you all this he had almost finished the crèche; the little houses were all in place, and the animals grouped about the holy stable, or else seeming to crop the tufts of moss on the mimic rocky hillside.

"Well, well!" said the Père Michaud, who had just entered the cottage, "'t is a fine bit of work thou hast there, my son! Truly 't is a brave crèche!"

But here the Misè called them both to the midday meal, which she had spread smoking hot on the shining deal table.

When this was finished Félix arose, and, as the Père wished, once more went out to the fold to see how the sheep, and especially his little Beppo, were faring.

As he pushed open the swinging door, Ninette, who was lazily dozing with her toes doubled up under her fleece, blinked her eyes and looked sleepily around; but Beppo was nowhere to be seen.

"Ninette!" demanded Félix fiercely, "what hast thou done with my Beppo?"

At this Ninette peered about in a dazed sort of way, and gave an alarmed little "Baa!" for she had not before missed Beppo, who, while she was asleep, had managed to push open the door of the fold and scamper off, no one knew just where.

Félix gazed around in dismay when he realized that his lamb, the chosen one, who had brought such pride and honor to him—that this was gone!

"Beppo!" he shouted at the top of his lungs, "Beppo! Beppo-o!"

But no trace could he see of the little bundle of fleece he had scrubbed and combed so carefully that morning.

He stood irresolute a moment; then, thinking that if Beppo really were running off, not a second was to be lost, he set out at a brisk pace across the sheep-meadow. He had no idea in what direction the truant lamb would be likely to stray, but on he went, calling every little while in a shrill voice, "Beppo!" Now and then he fancied that he saw in the distance a glimpse of white; but once it proved the Misè Fouchard's linen hung to dry on a currant-bush, and again it was a great white stone—but no

Beppo; and all the while Félix kept on, quite forgetting that Beppo's weak, woolly legs could not possibly have carried him so great a distance.

By and by he had left the village meadows far behind, and was skirting the great marsh. Sometimes he shaded his eyes with his hand and looked far across this low wet land to see if perhaps Beppo had strayed into its uncertain foothold; but nothing could he see but the waving rushes and the tall bitterns wading about on long, yellow legs.

And still he pressed heedlessly on farther and farther, till, after a while, he found himself thrusting through a thick coppice of willow boughs. "Oh," thought Félix, "what if poor Beppo has strayed into this woodland!" And tired as he was, he urged himself on, searching among the trees; and it was not until he had wandered on and on, deeper and deeper into the wood, that he realized that the dusk had fallen, and that he must be a very, very long way from Sur Varne.

Félix then began to grow uneasy. He stood still and looked anxiously about him; the dark forest trees closed around him on all sides, and he was quite unable to remember from which direction he had entered the wood.

Now, Félix was really a very brave little fellow, but he fairly quaked as he peered through the gathering darkness; for in those days the forests of Provence were known to harbor many dangerous animals, especially wild boars and wolves. He pricked up his ears, and now and then thought he heard in the distance the stealthy tread of some four-footed forest prowler, and once he was sure he caught the deep howl of a wolf.

That ended his hesitation. He looked quickly around, and grasping the low boughs of a slender sapling, managed to swing himself up into a tall chestnut-tree that grew close by; and there he clung, clutching the thick branches with might and main, feeling very cold and hungry and miserable, his heart all the while sinking clear down into his little peasant shoes.

And indeed he had cause for fear, for, not a great while after he had thus hidden himself, a gaunt wolf really did pass close by, sniffing and peering, till poor Félix fairly gave up all hope of escaping from the tree; but, luckily, the wolf did not see him, and at last slowly crept on through the underwood.

How long the little boy stayed in the perilous shelter of the chestnut-tree he never knew, but it seemed untold ages to him. After a while the moon rose, and shed a faint light through the close-lapping branches; and then, by and by, Félix's ears, strained to listen for every lightest sound, caught the echo of distant tramping, as of horses' hoofs, and presently two horsemen came in sight, picking their way cautiously along a narrow bridle-path.

He did not know whom they might prove to be, but wisely thinking that anything would be better than staying in a tree all night at the mercy of hungry wolves, he waited till the first rider came quite close, and then he plucked up courage to call out faintly: "Oh, sir, stop, I pray thee!"

At this, the rider, who was none other than the noble Count Bernard of Bois Varne, quickly drew rein and, turning, called to his companion:

"Ho, Brian! Heardest thou aught?"

"Nay, my lord," answered Brian, who was some paces behind, "naught save the trampling of our own horses' hoofs."

The count looked all around, and seeing nothing, thought himself mistaken in the sound, and began to pace on. Then Félix, in terror, gave another shout, this time louder, and at the same moment a little twig he was pressing with his elbow broke away and dropped, striking against the count's stirrup; for the bridle-path wound directly under the tree where Félix was perched.

The count instantly checked his horse again, and, peering up into the boughs overhead, he caught sight of Félix, his yellow hair wet with dew and shining in the moonlight, and his dark eyes wide with fear.

"Heigh-ho!" exclaimed the count, in blank amazement. "Upon my word, now! what art thou—boy or goblin?"

At this Félix gave a little sob, for he was very tired and very cold. He hugged the tree tightly, and, steadying himself against the boughs, at last managed to falter out: "Please thee, sir, I am Félix Michaud, and my lamb Beppo, who was to ride in the Christmas procession, ran off to-day, and—and—I have been hunting him, I think, ever since—since yesterday!" Here poor Félix grew a trifle bewildered; it seemed to him so very long ago since he had set out in search of Beppo. "And I live in Sur Varne."

At this the count gave a long whistle. "At Sur Varne!" he exclaimed. "If thou speakest truly, my little man, thou hast indeed a sturdy pair of legs to have carried thee thus far." And he eyed curiously Félix's dusty little feet and leathern leggings, dangling limply from the bough above him. "Dost thou know how far distant is Sur Varne from this forest?"

"Nay, sir," answered Félix; "but I trow 't is a great way."

"There thou art right," said the count; "'t is a good two leagues, if it is a pace. But how now? Thou canst not bide here to become the prey of hungry wolves, my little night-owl of the yellow hair!"

And thereupon Count Bernard dexterously raised himself in his stirrups, and, reaching upward, caught Félix in his arms and swung him down plump on the saddle-bow in front of him; then, showing him how to steady himself by holding the pommel, he turned to Brian, his squire, who while all this was going on had stood by in silent astonishment, and giving the order to move, the little cavalcade hastened on at a rapid pace in order to get clear of the forest as quickly as possible.

Meantime the Count Bernard, who was really a very kind and noble lord, and who lived in a beautiful castle on the farther verge of the forest, quite reassured Félix by talking to him kindly, and telling him of the six days' journey from which he and his squire Brian were just returning, and how they had been delayed on the way until nightfall.

"And, by my faith!" said Count Bernard, "thou shalt sleep this night in the strong castle of Bois Varne, with not even a mouse to fret thy yellow head; and, what is more, thou shalt see the fairest little maid that ever thou hast set eyes on!"

And then he told him of his little daughter, the Lady Elinor, and how she would play with Félix and show him the castle, and how on the morrow they would see about sending him home to Sur Varne.

And all the while the count was talking they were trotting briskly onward, till by and by they emerged from the forest and saw towering near at hand the castle of Bois Varne. The tall turrets shone and shimmered in the moonlight, and over the gateway of the drawbridge hung a lighted cresset— that is, a beautiful wrought-iron basket, in which blazed a ruddy torch of oil to light them on their way.

At sight of this the count and Brian spurred on their horses, and were soon clattering across the bridge and into the great paved courtyard. The count flung his bridle to a little page who hastened out to meet him, and then, springing from his saddle, lightly lifted Félix and swung him to the ground. He took the boy by the hand and led him into the great hall of the castle.

To Félix this looked marvelously beautiful. Christmas garlands of myrtle hung on the walls, and a great pile of freshly cut laurel boughs lay on a bench, ready for the morrow's arranging. But that which took his eyes most of all was the lovely carving everywhere to be seen. The benches and tables were covered with it; the wainscot of the spacious room was richly adorned; and over and about the wide fireplace great carved dragons of stone curled their long tails and spread their wings through a maze of intricate traceries. Félix was enchanted, and gazed around till his eyes fairly ached.

Presently in came running a little girl, laughing with delight. Bounding up into Count Bernard's arms, she hugged and kissed him in true Provençal fashion. Then, catching sight of Félix, "Ah, mon père," she exclaimed, "and where foundest thou thy pretty new page?"

"Nay, sweetheart," answered the count, looking down at Félix's yellow hair; "'t is no page, but a little goldfinch we found perched in a chestnut-tree as we rode through the forest."

Then, smiling at the Lady Elinor's bewilderment, he told her the little boy's story, and she at once slipped down and greeted him kindly. Then, clapping her hands with pleasure at finding a new playmate, she declared he must come and see the Christmas crèche which she was just finishing. She seized him by the hand and hastened across the hall, where her crèche was built up on a carved bench. The poor little Lady Elinor had no mother, and her father, the count, had been gone for several days; and while in the castle were no end of serving men and women and retainers, yet none of these presumed to dictate to the little mistress, and so she had put her crèche together in a very odd fashion.

"There!" said she, "what thinkest thou of it, Félix? Of a truth, I fancy somewhat is wanting, yet I know not how to better it!"

"Yes," said Felix, bashfully; "it may be I can help thee."

And so he set to work rearranging the little houses and figures, till he succeeded in giving quite a lifelike air to the crèche, and Lady Elinor fairly danced with delight.

While placing the little manger he happened to remember the figure of the Christ Child still in his blouse pocket; this he timidly took out and showed the little girl, who was charmed, and still more so when he drew forth a small wooden sheep and a dog, which were also in the same pocket.

The Lady Elinor was so carried away with joy that she flew to the side of the count, and, grasping both his hands, dragged him across the room to show him the crèche and the wonderful figures carved by Félix.

"See, mon père!" said Elinor, "see this, and this!" And she held up the little carvings for the count's inspection.

Count Bernard, who had good-naturedly crossed the room to please his little daughter, now opened his eyes wide with surprise. He took the little figures she handed him and examined them closely, for he was a good judge of artistic work of this kind. Then he looked at Félix, and at length he said:

"Well, little forest bird, who taught thee the carver's craft?"

"No one, sir," faltered Félix; "indeed, I wish, above all things, to learn of the Père Videau, the master carver; but my father says I must be a shepherd, as he is."

Here a tear rolled down Félix's cheek, for you must remember he was terribly tired.

"Well, well," said the count, "never mind! Thou art weary, little one; we will talk of this more on the morrow. 'T is high time now that both of you were sound asleep. Hey, there! Jean! Jacques! Come hither and take care of this little lad, and see to it that he hath a soft bed and a feather pillow!"

The next morning the children ate a merry breakfast together, and after it Count Bernard took Félix aside and asked him many questions of his life and his home. Then, by and by, knowing how anxious the boy's parents would be, he ordered his trusty squire, Brian, to saddle a horse and conduct Félix back to Sur Varne.

Meantime the little Lady Elinor begged hard that he stay longer in the castle for her playfellow, and was quite heartbroken when she saw the horse stand ready in the courtyard. Indeed, she would not be satisfied until her father, the count, who could not bear to see her unhappy, had promised to some day take her over to see Félix in Sur Varne. Then she smiled, and made a pretty farewell courtesy, and suddenly snatching from her dark hair a crimson ribbon of Lyons taffeta, she tied it about Félix's sleeve, declaring, "There! thou must keep this token, and be my little knight!" for the Lady Elinor had many lofty notions in her small curly head.

Félix could only stammer out an embarrassed good-by, for in the presence of this lively little maid he found himself quaking more than when he feared the terrible wolves of the forest. In another moment Brian lifted him to the saddle, and, springing up behind, took the bridle-rein, and off they went.

When, after several hours' riding, they drew near Sur Varne, Félix showed Brian the way to the Michaud cottage, and you can fancy how overjoyed were the Père and Misè to see the travelers; for they had been fairly beside themselves with grief, and had searched all night for their little son.

Of course almost the first question Félix asked was about Beppo, and he felt a great load taken off his mind when he learned that the little truant, who had not really strayed very far from the village, had been found and brought home by one of the shepherds, and was even then penned up safe and sound in the sheepfold.

After a good night's sleep Félix was quite rested from his journey, and was busy the next day in helping garland the Yule log, in giving Ninette and Beppo an extra scrubbing and brushing, and in all the final happy preparations for the great holiday.

And so Christmas Eve came. It was a lovely star-lit night, and on all sides one could hear the beautiful Christmas songs of old Provence that all the peasants and the children sang as they trooped along the roads on their way to the great church of the village; for thither every one flocked as the expected hour drew on.

Then presently the stately service began, and went on with song and incense, and the sweet chanting of children's voices, till suddenly from the upper tower of the church a joyous peal of bells rang in the midnight! And all at once, through the dense throng of worshipers nearest the door a pathway opened, and in came four peasants playing on pipes and flutes and flageolets a quaint old air made up three hundred years before by good King René for just such a ceremony as was to follow.

After the pipers walked ten shepherds, two by two, each wearing a long brown cloak, and carrying a staff and lighted candle; that is, all save the first two, and these bore, one a basket of fruit, the melons and grapes and pears of sunny Provence, while the other held in his hands a pair of pretty white pigeons with rose-colored eyes and soft, fluttering wings.

And then, behind the shepherds came—what do you suppose?—Ninette! Ninette, her fleece shining like snow, a garland of laurel and myrtle about her neck, and twigs of holly nodding behind her ears, while bound about her woolly shoulders a little harness of scarlet leather shone against the white with dazzling effect; and fastened to the harness, and trundling along at Ninette's heels, came the gayest of little wooden carts. It was painted in the brightest colors. Its wheels were wrapped with garlands, and in it, curled up in a fat fleecy ball, lay Beppo! Tied about his neck in a huge bow was a crimson ribbon of Lyons taffeta, with a sprig of holly tucked into its loops.

Beppo lay quite still, looking about him with a bewildered, half-dazed expression, and just behind his cart came ten more shepherds with staffs and candles, while following them was a great throng of peasant folk and children (among them Félix), all carrying lighted tapers, and radiant with delight; for this was the Procession of the Offered Lamb, and to walk in its train was considered by all as the greatest honor and privilege.

And especially did the shepherd folk love the beautiful old custom which for centuries the people of Provence had cherished from year to year in memory of the time, long ago, when the real Christ Child lay in the manger of Bethlehem, and the shepherds of Judea sought him out to worship him, and to offer him their fruits and lambs as gifts.

And so on up the long aisle the procession slowly moved, the pipers playing, and Ninette marching solemnly along, only now and then pausing to thrust her nose between the Père Michaud and his companion, who walked directly in front of her. Ninette pattered on as if she had trod the floors of churches all her life; and as for Beppo, only once did he stir, and then he gave a faint "Baa!" and tried to uncurl himself and stand up; but just then the queer little cart gave a joggle which quite upset his shaky lamb legs, and down he sank, and kept quiet throughout the rest of the time.

After the service the players again struck up King René's tune, and the procession, shepherds, Ninette, Beppo, peasants, and all, once more moved on, this time down the outer aisle and toward the great open portal.

It took some time for the last of its followers to reach the doorway, for the throng was very great; but at length Félix, who had marched with the children in the last group, came to the threshold and stepped out into the starry night.

He stood for a moment smiling and gazing aimlessly ahead, overwhelmed with the glory of all that had passed within the church, when presently he felt some one pluck his sleeve, and turning round, he met the dancing eyes of the little Lady Elinor.

She gave a little peal of laughter at his surprise, and exclaimed: "Oh, I coaxed mon père, the count, to fetch me hither for this blessed night. Thou knowest he promised! I rode my white palfrey all the way by the side of his big brown horse. And I have seen the procession, and Beppo with my red ribbon round his neck." Here she gave another little gurgle of delight. "And oh, Félix, my father hath seen thine, and 't is all settled! Thou art to be a famous carver with the Père Videau, as thou wishest" (for the Lady Elinor had unbounded faith in Félix's powers); "and, Félix," she added, "I trow 't was the little Christ Child for thy crèche that did it!"

Then, with a merry little smile, she darted off to her father, the Count Bernard, who was waiting for her down the church path.

For a little while after she had gone Félix did not move, but stood as one in a dream. Presently a loud bleat close at his side startled him, and, looking down, he saw that Ninette, decked in her gay garlands, and still dragging the be-ribboned Beppo in the little cart, had broken away from the Père Michaud and come close up to himself.

Then, with a sudden movement, he stooped over, and, seizing Beppo in both arms, hugged and squeezed him till poor Beppo squeaked with surprise, and opened his red mouth and fairly gasped for breath. But Félix only hugged him the harder, murmuring under his breath, "Bless thy little heart, Beppo! Bless thy little heart!" For in a vague way he realized that the truant lamb had somehow brought him his heart's desire, and that was quite enough Christmas happiness for one year.

And the little Lady Elinor was right, too. Years after, when Félix grew to be a man, he did, in very truth, become a "famous carver," as she had declared.

Far surpassing his first master, the Père Videau, he traveled and worked in many cities; yet never, through all his long life, did he forget that Christmas Eve in the little village of Sur Varne.

Those who knew him best said that among his dearest treasures he always kept a beautifully carved little box, and in it a bit of faded crimson ribbon from the looms of Lyons. While, as for Beppo—well, if ever some happy day you chance to visit the lovely land of Provence, perhaps you will see a certain grand old cathedral in the ancient city of Arles; and, if you do, look sharp at the figure of a lamb chiseled in white stone over the great portal. Look well, I say, for Félix, when he carved it, would have told you that he was thinking all the while of his little pet lamb Beppo.

THE SABOT OF LITTLE WOLFF

FRANÇOIS COPPÉE

Once upon a time,—it was so long ago that the whole world has forgotten the date,—in a city in the north of Europe, whose name is so difficult to pronounce that nobody remembers it,—once upon a time there was a little boy of seven, named Wolff. He was an orphan in charge of an old aunt who was hard and avaricious, who only kissed him on New Year's Day, and who breathed a sigh of regret every time that she gave him a porringer of soup.

But the poor little lad was naturally so good that he loved his aunt just the same, although she frightened him very much; and he could never see her without trembling, for fear she would whip him.

As the aunt of Wolff was known through all the village to have a house and an old stocking full of gold, she did not dare send her nephew to the school for the poor, but she obtained a reduction of the price with the schoolmaster whose school little Wolff attended. The teacher, vexed at having a scholar so badly dressed and who paid so poorly, often punished him unjustly, and even set his fellow-pupils against him.

The poor little fellow was therefore as miserable as the stones in the street, and hid himself in out-of-the-way corners to cry when Christmas came.

The night before Christmas the schoolmaster was to take all of his pupils to church, and bring them back to their homes. As the winter was very severe that year, and as for several days a great quantity of snow had fallen, the children came to the master's house warmly wrapped and bundled up, with fur caps pulled down over their ears, double and triple jackets, knitted gloves and mittens, and good, thick-nailed boots with strong soles. Only little Wolff came shivering in the clothes that he wore week-days and Sundays, and with nothing on his feet but coarse Strasbourg socks and heavy sabots, or wooden shoes.

His thoughtless comrades made a thousand jests over his forlorn looks and his peasant's dress; but little Wolff was so occupied in blowing on his fingers to keep them warm, that he took no notice of the boys or what they said.

The troop of boys, with their master at their head, started for the church. As they went they talked of the fine suppers that were waiting them at home. The son of the burgomaster had seen, before he went out, a monstrous goose that the truffles marked with black spots like a leopard. At the house of one of the boys there was a little fir tree in a wooden box, from whose branches hung oranges, sweetmeats and toys.

The children spoke, too, of what the Christ-child would bring to them, and what he would put in their shoes, which they would, of course, be very careful to leave in the chimney before going to bed. And the eyes of those little boys, lively as a parcel of mice, sparkled in advance with the joy of seeing in their imagination pink paper bags filled with cakes, lead soldiers drawn up in battalions in their boxes, menageries smelling of varnished wood, and magnificent jumping-jacks covered with purple and bells.

Little Wolff knew very well by experience that his old aunt would send him supperless to bed; but, knowing that all the year he had been as good and industrious as possible, he hoped that the Christ-child would not forget him, and he, too, looked eagerly forward to putting his wooden shoes in the ashes of the fireplace.

When the service was ended, every one went away, anxious for his supper, and the band of children, walking two by two after their teacher, left the church.

In the porch, sitting on a stone seat under a Gothic niche, a child was sleeping—a child who was clad in a robe of white linen, and whose feet were bare, notwithstanding the cold. He was not a beggar, for his robe was new and fresh, and near him on the ground was seen a square, a hatchet, a pair of compasses, and the other tools of a carpenter's apprentice. Under the light of the stars, his face bore an expression of divine sweetness, and his long locks of golden hair seemed like an aureole about his head. But the child's feet, blue in the cold of that December night, were sad to see.

The children, so well clothed and shod for the winter, passed heedlessly before the unknown child. One of them, the son of one of the principal men in the village, looked at the waif with an expression in which no pity could be seen.

But little Wolff, coming the last out of the church, stopped, full of compassion, before the beautiful sleeping child. "Alas!" said the orphan to himself, "it is too bad that this poor little one has to go barefoot in such bad weather. But what is worse than all, he has not even a boot or a wooden shoe to leave before him while he sleeps to-night, so that the Christ-child could put something there to comfort him in his misery."

And, carried away by the goodness of his heart, little Wolff took off the wooden shoe from his right foot, and laid it in front of the sleeping child. Then, limping along on his poor blistered foot and dragging his sock through the snow, he went back to his aunt's house.

"Look at that worthless fellow!" cried his aunt, full of anger at his return without one of his shoes. "What have you done with your wooden shoe, little wretch?"

Little Wolff did not know how to deceive, and although he was shaking with terror, he tried to stammer out some account of his adventure.

The old woman burst into a frightful peal of laughter. "Ah, monsieur takes off his shoes for beggars! Ah, monsieur gives away his wooden shoes to a barefoot! This is something new! Ah, well, since that is so, I am going to put the wooden shoe which you have left in the chimney, and I promise you the Christ-child will leave there to-night something to whip you with in the morning. And you shall pass the day to-morrow on dry bread and water. We will see if next time you give away your shoe to the first vagabond that comes."

Then the aunt, after having given the poor boy a couple of slaps, made him climb up to his bed in the attic. Grieved to the heart, the child went to bed in the dark, and soon went to sleep, his pillow wet with tears.

On the morrow morning, when the old woman went downstairs—oh, wonderful sight!—she saw the great chimney full of beautiful playthings, and sacks of magnificent candies, and all sorts of good things; and before all these splendid things the right shoe, that her nephew had given to the little waif, stood by the side of the left shoe, that she herself had put there that very night, and where she meant to put a birch rod.

As little Wolff, running down to learn the meaning of his aunt's exclamation, stood in artless ecstasy before all these splendid gifts, suddenly there were loud cries and laughter out of doors. The old woman and the little boy went out to know what it all meant, and saw the neighbors gathered around the public fountain. What had happened? Oh, something very amusing and extraordinary! The children of all the rich people of the village, those whose parents had wished to surprise them with the most beautiful gifts, had found only rods in their shoes.

Then the orphan and the old woman, thinking of all the beautiful things that were in their chimney, were full of amazement. But presently they saw the curé coming toward them, with wonder in his face. In the church porch, where in the evening a child, clad in a white robe, and with bare feet, had rested his sleeping head, the curé had just seen a circle of gold incrusted with precious stones.

Then the people understood that the beautiful sleeping child, near whom were the carpenter's tools, was the Christ-child in person, become for an hour such as he was when he worked in his parents' house, and they bowed themselves before that miracle that the good God had seen fit to work, to reward the faith and charity of a child.

THE LITTLE FRIEND

ABBIE FARWELL BROWN

"Oh! I am so cold, so cold!" sobbed little Pierre, as he stumbled through the snow which was drifting deep upon the mountain side. "Oh, I am so cold! The snow bites my face and blinds me, so that I cannot see the road. Where are all the Christmas candle-lights? The people of the village must have forgotten. The little Jesus will lose His way to-night. I never forgot to set our window at home full of lights on Christmas Eve. But now it is Christmas Eve, and there is no home any more. And I am so cold, so cold!"

Little Pierre sobbed again and stumbled in the snow, which was drifting deeper and deeper upon the mountain side. This was the stormiest Christmas Eve which had been seen for years, and all the little boys who had good homes were hugging themselves close to the fire, glad that they were not out in the bleak night. Every window was full of flickering tapers to light the expected Holy Child upon His way through the village to the church. But little Pierre had strayed so far from the road that he could not see these rows and rows of tiny earth-stars, any more than he could see through the snow the far-off sky-stars which the angels had lighted along the streets of heaven.

Pierre was on his way to the village from the orphan boys' home at the Abbé's charity school. And that was not like a happy real home, for the little Brothers were rough and rude and far from loving one another. He had started at dusk from the school, hoping to be at the village church before curfew. For Pierre had a sweet little voice, and he was to earn a few pennies by singing in the choir on Christmas morning. But it was growing late. The church would be closed and the Curé gone home before Pierre could reach it; and then what should he do?

The snow whirled faster and faster, and Pierre's legs found it harder and harder to move themselves through the great drifts. They seemed heavy and numb, and he was growing oh, so tired! If he could but lie down to sleep until Christmas Day! But he knew that he must not do that. For those who choose this kind of soft and tempting bed turn into ice-people, and do not wake up in the morning. So he bent his head and tried to plough on through the drifts.

Whish! A soft white thing flapped through the snow and struck Pierre in the face, so that he staggered and almost lost his balance. The next moment he had caught the thing as it fell and was holding it tenderly in his numb hands. It was a beautiful dove, white as the snow from which it seemed to come. It had been whirled about by the storm until it had lost strength to fly, and it now lay quite still, with closed eyes. Pierre stroked the ruffled feathers gently and blew upon its cold body, trying to bring it back to life.

"Poor bird!" he said softly. "You are lost in the snow, like me. I will try to keep you warm, though I am myself a cold little body." He put the bird under his jacket, holding it close to his heart. Presently the dove opened its eyes and stirred feebly, giving a faint "Coo!"

"I wish I had something for you to eat, poor bird," said Pierre, forgetting his own cold and hunger. "If I could but take you into my own house and feed you as I used to feed the birds upon Christmas Eve! But now I have no home myself, and I can scarcely keep you warm."

Pierre shivered and tried to move forward. But the storm seemed to grow even fiercer, and the wind blew so keenly in his face that he could scarcely stand. "I cannot go another step," he said, and down he sank in the snow, which began to cover him with a downy blanket, pretending to be a careful mother. He hugged the bird closer and began to feel afraid. He knew that he was in great danger. "Dear Dove," he whispered, "I am sorry that I cannot save you. We shall turn into ice-images together. But I will keep you warm as long as I can." Then he closed his eyes, for he was very sleepy.

In a little while something made Pierre open his eyes. At first he could see only the whirling snow, which seemed to be everywhere. But presently he found that some one was bending over him, with face close to his; some one chubby and rosy and young,—a child like himself, but more beautiful than any child whom Pierre had ever seen. He stared hard at the face which seemed to smile at him through the snow, not minding the cold.

"You have my dove inside your coat," said the Child, pointing. "I lost her in the storm. Give her to me."

Pierre held his coat the closer. "She was cold," he answered. "She was dying in the snow. I am trying to keep her warm."

"But she is warm when she is with me, though I have no coat to wrap her in," said the Child. And, indeed, he was clad only in a little shirt, with his rosy legs quite bare. Yet he looked not cold. A brightness glowed about him, and his breath seemed to warm the air. Pierre saw that, though it was still snowing beyond them, there were no whirling flakes between him and the Child.

The little Stranger held out his hand once more. "Please give me the dove," he begged. "I must hasten on my way to the village yonder. The dove strayed from my bosom and was lost. You found her here, far from the road. Thank you, little boy. Are you often so kind to poor lost birds!"

"Why, they are the Lord's own birds!" cried little Pierre. "How should one not be kind and love them dearly? On the Lord's birthday eve, too! It is little that I could do for this one,—I who have saved and fed so many on other Christmas Eves. Alas, I wish I was back in those good old days of the wheat-sheaf and the full pan of milk and the bright warm fire!" Pierre's eyes filled with tears.

"What! Did you set a sheaf of wheat for the birds on Christmas Eve?" asked the Child, drawing closer and bending kindly eyes upon Pierre.

Now the boy saw that where the Stranger stood the snow had melted all away, so that they were inclosed in a little space like a downy nest, which seemed almost warm to his limbs.

"Yes, I set out a wheat-sheaf," said Pierre simply. "Why not? I love all the little creatures whom our Lord Himself so dearly loved, and to whom He bade us be kind. On Christmas Eve especially I always tried to make happy those which He sent in my way,—poor little wanderers as well as our own friends at home."

The Child drew yet closer and sat down in the snow beside Pierre. His beautiful eyes shone like stars, and his voice was like sweet music. "What," he said, "you are the boy who stood in the doorway with a pan of bread and milk,—part of your own supper,—and called the hungry kitten to feast? You are the same who tossed a bone to the limping dog and made him a bed in the stable? You stroked the noses of the ox and the ass and said gentle things to them, because they were the first friends of the little Jesus? You set the sheaf of wheat for the snow-birds, and they lighted upon your hands and shoulders and kissed your lips in gratitude? You are that boy, friend of God's friends. No wonder that my white dove flew to you out of the storm. She knew, she knew!"

The Child bent near and kissed Pierre on the cheeks, so that they grew rosy, and the warm blood went tingling through his little cold limbs. Sitting up, he said: "Yes, I am that boy who last year was so happy because he could do these pleasant things. But how do you know, little Stranger? How did you see?"

"Oh, I know, I saw!" cried the Child, gleefully clapping his hands as a child will. "I was there. I passed through the village last Christmas Eve, and I saw it all. But tell me now, how do you come here, dear boy? Why are you not in that happy home this stormy night, once more making the Lord's creatures happy?"

Pierre told all to the Child: how his dear father and mother had died and left him alone in the world; how the home had been sold, and now he lived in the charity school kept by the good Abbé; how he had learned of the chance to earn a few pennies by singing on Christmas Day in the neighboring village church, which lacked a voice among the choir-boys; how he was on his way thither when the storm had hidden the road, and he had grown so cold, so cold!

"Then your dove came to me, little Stranger," Pierre concluded. "She came, and I folded her in my jacket to keep her warm. But, do you know, it must be that she has kept me warm. Although I could walk no further, I am not cold at all, nor frightened, and no longer hungry. Sit close to me, little Stranger. You shall share my jacket, too, and we will all three warm one another."

The Child laughed again, a low, soft, silvery laugh, like a happy brook slipping over the pebbles. "I am not cold," he said. "I cannot stay with you. I must go yonder." And he pointed through the snow.

"Whither, oh, whither?" cried Pierre eagerly. "Let me go with you. I am lost; but if you know the way we can go together, hand in hand."

The Child shook his head. "Not so," he said. "I do not follow the path, and your feet would stumble. I shall find a way without sinking in the snow. I must go alone. But there is a better way for you. I leave my dove with you: she will keep you warm until help comes. Farewell, friend of the Lord's friends." Stooping the Child kissed Pierre once more, upon the forehead. Then, before the boy saw how he went, he had vanished from the little nest of snow, without leaving a footprint behind.

Now the dove, clasped close to Pierre's heart, seemed to warm him like a little fire within; and the Child's kiss on his forehead made him so happy, but withal so drowsy, that he smiled as he closed his eyes once more repeating, "'Until help comes.' 'There is a better way' for me."

On the side of the mountain, away from the village street, perched the little hut of Grandfather Viaud. And here, on Christmas Eve, sat the old man and his wife, looking very sad and lonely. For there was no sound of childish laughter in the little hut, no patter of small feet, no whispering of Christmas secrets. The little Viauds had long since grown up and flown away to build nests of their own in far-off countries. Poor Josef Viaud and old Bettine were quite alone this Christmas Eve, save for the Saint Bernard who was stretched out before the fire, covering half the floor with his huge bulk, like a furry rug. He was the very Prince of dogs, as his name betokened, and he was very good to Grandfather and Grandmother, who loved him dearly. But on Christmas Eve even the littlest cottage, crowded with the biggest tenants, seems lonely unless there are children in the corners.

The Viauds sat silently gazing into the fire, with scarcely a word for each other, scarcely a caress for faithful Prince. Indeed, the great dog himself seemed to know that something was lacking, and every once in a while would lift his head and whine wistfully.

In each of the two small windows burned a row of candles, flickering in the draught that blew down the great chimney and swept through the little chamber. And these, with the crackling blaze upon the hearth, sent queer shadows quivering up the smoky walls.

Grandfather Viaud looked over his shoulder as a great gust blew the ashes into the room. "Hey!" he cried. "I almost fancied the shadow of one looking in at the window. Ha, ha! What foolishness! Eh! but it is a fearsome storm. Pray the good Lord that there may be no poor creatures wandering on the mountain this night."

"The Lord's birthday, too!" said Grandmother Bettine. "The dear little Child has a cold way to come. Even He might become confused and be driven to wander by such a whirl of snow. I am glad that we set the tapers there, Josef, even though we be so far from the village street down which they say He passes. How pleasant to think that one might give light to His blessed feet if they were wandering from the way,—the dear little Child's feet, so rosy and soft and tender!" And good Grandmother Viaud dropped a tear upon her knitting; for she remembered many such little feet that had once pattered about the cottage floor. Prince lifted his head and seemed to listen, then whined as he had done before.

"You are lonely, old fellow, are you not?" quavered old Josef. "You are waiting for the children to come back and make it merry, as it used to be in the old days when you were a pup. Heigho! Those were pleasant days, but they will never come again, Prince. We are all growing old, we three together."

"Ah, peace, Josef, peace!" cried old Bettine, wiping her eyes again. "It is lonely enough and sad enough, God knows, without speaking of it. What use to sigh for that which cannot be? If the good Lord wished us to have a comforter in our old age, doubtless He would send us one. He knows how we have longed and prayed that a child's feet might echo through our house once more: how we have hoped from year to year that one of the grandchildren might return to bless us with his little presence." At this moment Prince jumped to his feet with a low bark, and stood trembling, with pointed ears.

"What dost thou hear, old dog?" asked the Grandfather carelessly. "There is naught human abroad this night, I warrant you. All wise folk are hugging the fire like us. Only those bad spirits of Christmas Eve are howling about for mischief, they say. Best keep away from the door, old Prince, lest they nip your toes or bite your nose for spite."

"Hush!" cried the Grandmother, laying her hand upon his arm. "You forget: there is the Other One abroad. It may be that He—"

She was interrupted by Prince, who ran eagerly to the door and began sniffing at the latch in great excitement. Then he gave a long, low howl. At the same moment the latch rattled, and the Viauds distinctly heard a little voice cry, "Open, open, good people!"

The old couple looked at each other; the cheeks of one flushed, and the other's paled. At the same moment they rose stiffly from their chairs by the fire. But Grandmother Bettine was first at the door. She lifted the latch, the door blew open violently, and with a loud bark Prince dashed out into the storm.

"What is it? Who is there?" cried Josef Viaud, peering over his wife's shoulder. But no one answered save the rough storm, which fiercely blew into the faces of the old couple, whirling and screaming about their heads. "H'm! It was only a fancy," muttered the old man. "Come in, Mother. Come, Prince!" and he whistled out into the storm. But the wind whistled too, drowning his voice, and Prince did not return. "He is gone!" cried Josef impatiently. "It is some evil spirit's work."

"Nay, Father!" and, as she spoke, the door banged violently in Josef's face, as if to emphasize the good wife's rebuke. "It was a little child; I heard it," insisted Bettine, as they staggered back to the fire and sank weakly into their chairs. "Perhaps it was the Holy Child Himself, who knows? But why would He not enter? Why, Josef! Oh, I fear we were not good enough!"

"I only know that we have perhaps lost our good dog. Why did you open the door, Bettine?" grumbled Josef sleepily.

"Prince is not lost. For what was he bred a snow-dog upon the mountains if a storm like this be danger to him? He is of the race that rescues, that finds and is never lost. Mayhap the Holy Child had work for him this night. Ah, the Little One! If I could but have seen Him for one moment!" And good Bettine's head nodded drowsily on her chair-back. Presently the old couple were fast asleep.

Now when they had been dreaming strange things for some time, there came a scratching at the door, and a loud bark which woke them suddenly.

"What was that?" exclaimed Grandfather, starting nervously. "Ho, Prince! Are you without there?" and he ran to the door, while Grandmother was still rubbing from her eyes the happy dream which had made them moist,—the dream of a rosy, radiant Child who was to be the care and comfort of a lonely cottage. And then, before she had fairly wakened from the dream, Prince bounded into the room and laid before the fire at her feet a soft, snow-wrapped bundle, from which hung a pale little face with golden hair.

"It is the Child of my dream!" cried Bettine. "The Holy One has come back to us."

"Nay, this is no dream-child, mother. This is a little human fellow, nearly frozen to death," exclaimed Josef Viaud, pulling the bundle toward the fire. "Come, Bettine, let us take off his snow-stiff clothes and get some little garments from the chests yonder. I will give him a draught of something warm, and rub the life into his poor little hands and feet. We have both been dreaming, it seems. But certainly this is no dream!"

"Look! The dove!" cried Grandmother, taking the bird from the child's bosom, where it still nestled, warm and warming. "Josef! I believe it is indeed the Holy Child Himself," she whispered. "He bears a dove in his bosom, like the image in the Church." But even as she spoke the dove fluttered in her fingers, then, with a gentle "Coo-roo!" whirled once about the little chamber and darted out at the door, which they had forgotten quite to close. With that the child opened his eyes.

"The dove is gone!" he cried. "Yet I am warm. Why—has the little Stranger come once more?" Then he saw the kind old faces bent over him, and felt Prince's warm kisses on his hands and cheeks, with the fire flickering pleasantly beyond.

"It is like coming home again!" he murmured, and with his head on Bettine's shoulder dropped comfortably to sleep.

On the morrow all the village went to see the image of the Christ Child lying in a manger near the high altar of the church. It was a sweet little Child in a white shirt, clasping in his hands a dove. They believed him to have come in the stormy night down the village street. And they were glad that their pious candles in the windows had guided Him safely on the road. But little Pierre, while he sang in the choir, and his adopted parents, the Viauds, kneeling happily below, had sweet thoughts of a dream which had brought them all together.

Who knows but that Prince at home happily guarding Pierre's snow-wet old shoes—who knows but that Prince was dreaming the happiest dream of all? For only Prince knew how and where and under what guidance he had found the little friend of the Lord's friends sleeping in the snow, with but a white dove in his bosom to keep him from becoming a boy of ice.

WHERE LOVE IS, THERE GOD IS ALSO

COUNT LYOF N. TOLSTOÏ

In a certain city dwelt Martin Avdyeeich, the cobbler. He lived in a cellar, a wretched little hole with a single window. The window looked up towards the street, and through it Martin could just see the passers-by. It is true that he could see little more than their boots, but Martin Avdyeeich could read a man's character by his boots, so he needed no more. Martin Avdyeeich had lived long in that one place, and had many acquaintances. Few indeed were the boots in that neighborhood which had not passed through his hands at some time or other. On some he would fasten new soles, to others he would give side-pieces, others again he would stitch all round, and even give them new uppers if need be. And often he saw his own handiwork through the window. There was always lots of work for him, for Avdyeeich's hand was cunning and his leather good; nor did he overcharge, and he always kept his word. He always engaged to do a job by a fixed time if he could; but if he could not, he said so at once, and deceived no man. So every one knew Avdyeeich, and he had no lack of work. Avdyeeich had always been a pretty good man, but as he grew old he began to think more about his soul, and draw nearer to his God. While Martin was still a journeyman his wife had died; but his wife had left him a little boy—three years old. Their other children had not lived. All the eldest had died early. Martin wished at first to send his little child into the country to his sister, but afterwards he thought better of it. "My Kapitoshka," thought he, "will feel miserable in a strange household. He shall stay here with me." And so Avdyeeich left his master, and took to living in lodgings alone with his little son. But God did not give Avdyeeich happiness in his children. No sooner had the little one begun to grow up and be a help and a joy to his father's heart, than a sickness fell upon Kapitoshka, the little one took to his bed, lay there in a raging fever for a week, and then died. Martin buried his son in despair—so desperate was he that he began to murmur against God.

Such disgust of life overcame him that he more than once begged God that he might die; and he reproached God for taking not him, an old man, but his darling, his only son, instead. And after that Avdyeeich left off going to church.

And lo! one day, there came to Avdyeeich from the Troïtsa Monastery, an aged peasant-pilgrim—it was already the eighth year of his pilgrimage. Avdyeeich fell a-talking with him and began to complain of his great sorrow. "As for living any longer, thou man of God," said he, "I desire it not. Would only that I might die! That is my sole prayer to God. I am now a man who has no hope."

And the old man said to him: "Thy speech, Martin, is not good. How shall we judge the doings of God? God's judgments are not our thoughts. God willed that thy son shouldst die, but that thou shouldst live. Therefore 'twas the best thing both for him and for thee. It is because thou wouldst fain have lived for thy own delight that thou dost now despair."

"But what then *is* a man to live for?" asked Avdyeeich.

And the old man answered: "For God, Martin! He gave thee life, and for Him therefore must thou live. When thou dost begin to live for Him, thou wilt grieve about nothing more, and all things will come easy to thee."

Martin was silent for a moment, and then he said: "And how must one live for God?"

"Christ hath shown us the way. Thou knowest thy letters. Buy the Gospels and read; there thou wilt find out how to live for God. There everything is explained."

These words made the heart of Avdyeeich burn within him, and he went the same day and bought for himself a New Testament printed in very large type, and began to read.

Avdyeeich set out with the determination to read it only on holidays; but as he read, it did his heart so much good that he took to reading it every day. And the second time he read until all the kerosene in the lamp had burnt itself out, and for all that he could not tear himself away from the book. And so it was every evening. And the more he read, the more clearly he understood what God wanted of him, and how it behooved him to live for God; and his heart grew lighter and lighter continually. Formerly, whenever he lay down to sleep he would only sigh and groan, and think of nothing but Kapitoshka, but now he would only say to himself: "Glory to Thee! Glory to Thee, O Lord! Thy will be done!"

Henceforth the whole life of Avdyeeich was changed. Formerly, whenever he had a holiday, he would go to the tavern to drink tea, nor would he say no to a drop of brandy now and again. He would tipple with his comrades, and though not actually drunk, would, for all that, leave the inn a bit merry, babbling nonsense and talking loudly and censoriously. He had done with all that now. His life became quiet and joyful. With the morning light he sat down to his work, worked out his time, then took down his lamp from the hook, placed it on the table, took down his book from the shelf, bent over it, and sat him down to read. And the more he read the more he understood, and his heart grew brighter and happier.

It happened once that Martin was up reading till very late. He was reading St. Luke's Gospel. He was reading the sixth chapter, and as he read he came to the words: "And to him that smiteth thee on the one cheek, offer also the other." This passage he read several times, and presently he came to that place where the Lord says: "And why call ye me Lord, Lord, and do not the things which I say? Whosoever cometh to Me, and heareth My sayings, and doeth them, I will show you to whom he is like. He is like a man which built an house, and dug deep, and laid the foundations on a rock. And when the flood arose, the storm beat vehemently upon that house, and could not shake it, for it was founded upon a rock. But he that

---

heareth, and doeth not, is like a man that without a foundation built an house upon the earth, against which the stream did beat vehemently, and immediately it fell, and the ruin of that house was great."

Avdyeeich read these words through and through, and his heart was glad. He took off his glasses, laid them on the book, rested his elbow on the table, and fell a-thinking. And he began to measure his own life by these words. And he thought to himself, "Is my house built on the rock or on the sand? How good to be as on a rock! How easy it all seems to thee sitting alone here. It seems as if thou wert doing God's will to the full, and so thou takest no heed and fallest away again. And yet thou wouldst go on striving, for so it is good for thee. O Lord, help me!" Thus thought he, and would have laid him down, but it was a grief to tear himself away from the book. And so he began reading the seventh chapter. He read all about the Centurion, he read all about the Widow's Son, he read all about the answer to the disciples of St. John; and so he came to that place where the rich Pharisee invites our Lord to be his guest. And he read all about how the woman who was a sinner anointed His feet and washed them with her tears, and how He justified her. And so he came at last to the forty-fourth verse, and there he read these words, "And He turned to the woman and said to Simon, Seest thou this woman? I entered into thine house, thou gavest Me no water for My feet; but she has washed My feet with tears and wiped them with the hairs of her head. Thou gavest Me no kiss, but this woman, since the time I came in, hath not ceased to kiss My feet. Mine head with oil thou didst not anoint."

And again Avdyeeich took off his glasses, and laid them on the book, and fell a-thinking.

"So it is quite plain that I too have something of the Pharisee about me. Am I not always thinking of myself? Am I not always thinking of drinking tea, and keeping myself as warm and cozy as possible, without thinking at all about the guest? Simon thought about himself, but did not give the slightest thought to his guest. But who was the guest? The Lord Himself. And suppose He were to come to me, should I treat Him as the Pharisee did?"

And Avdyeeich leaned both his elbows on the table and, without perceiving it, fell a-dozing.

"Martin!"—it was as though the voice of some one close to his ear.

Martin started up from his nap. "Who's there?"

He turned round, he gazed at the door, but there was no one. Again he dozed off. Suddenly he heard quite plainly, "Martin, Martin, I say! Look to-morrow into the street. I am coming."

Martin awoke, rose from his chair, and began to rub his eyes. And he did not know himself whether he had heard these words asleep or awake. He turned down the lamp and laid him down to rest.

At dawn next day, Avdyeeich arose, prayed to God, lit his stove, got ready his gruel and cabbage soup, filled his samovar, put on his apron, and sat him down by his window to work. There Avdyeeich sits and works, and thinks of nothing but the things of yesternight. His thoughts were divided. He thought at one time that he must have gone off dozing, and then again he thought he really must have heard that voice. It might have been so, thought he.

Martin sits at the window and looks as much at his window as at his work, and whenever a strange pair of boots passes by he bends forward and looks out of the window, so as to see the face as well as the feet of the passers-by. The house porter passed by in new felt boots, the water-carrier passed by, and after that there passed close to the window an old soldier, one of Nicholas's veterans, in tattered old boots, with a shovel in his hands. Avdyeeich knew him by his boots. The old fellow was called

Stepanuich, and lived with the neighboring shopkeeper, who harbored him of his charity. His duty was to help the porter. Stepanuich stopped before Avdyeeich's window to sweep away the snow. Avdyeeich cast a glance at him, and then went on working as before.

"I'm not growing sager as I grow older," thought Avdyeeich, with some self-contempt. "I make up my mind that Christ is coming to me, and lo! 'tis only Stepanuich clearing away the snow. Thou simpleton, thou! thou art wool-gathering!" Then Avdyeeich made ten more stitches, and then he stretched his head once more towards the window. He looked through the window again, and there he saw that Stepanuich had placed the shovel against the wall, and was warming himself and taking breath a bit.

"The old man is very much broken," thought Avdyeeich to himself. "It is quite plain that he has scarcely strength enough to scrape away the snow. Suppose I make him drink a little tea! the samovar, too, is just on the boil." Avdyeeich put down his awl, got up, placed the samovar on the table, put some tea in it, and tapped on the window with his fingers. Stepanuich turned round and came to the window. Avdyeeich beckoned to him, and then went and opened the door.

"Come in and warm yourself a bit," cried he. "You're a bit chilled, eh?"

"Christ requite you! Yes, and all my bones ache too," said Stepanuich. Stepanuich came in, shook off the snow, and began to wipe his feet so as not to soil the floor, but he tottered sadly.

"Don't trouble about wiping your feet. I'll rub it off myself. It's all in the day's work. Come in and sit down," said Avdyeeich. "Here, take a cup of tea."

And Avdyeeich filled two cups, and gave one to his guest, and he poured his own tea out into the saucer and began to blow it.

Stepanuich drank his cup, turned it upside down, put a gnawed crust on the top of it, and said, "Thank you." But it was quite plain that he wanted to be asked to have some more.

"Have a drop more. Do!" said Avdyeeich, and poured out fresh cups for his guest and himself, and as Avdyeeich drank his cup, he could not help glancing at the window from time to time.

"Dost thou expect any one?" asked his guest.

"Do I expect any one? Well, honestly, I hardly know. I am expecting and I am not expecting, and there's a word which has burnt itself right into my heart. Whether it was a vision or no, I know not. Look now, my brother! I was reading yesterday about our little Father Christ, how He suffered, how He came on earth. Hast thou heard of Him, eh?"

"I have heard, I have heard," replied Stepanuich, "but we poor ignorant ones know not our letters."

"Anyhow, I was reading about this very thing—how He came down upon earth. I was reading how He went to the Pharisee, and how the Pharisee did not meet Him half-way. That was what I was reading about yesternight, little brother mine. I read that very thing, and bethought me how the Honorable did not receive our little Father Christ honorably. But suppose, I thought, if He came to one like me—would I receive Him? Simon at any rate did not receive Him at all. Thus I thought, and so thinking, fell asleep. I fell asleep, I say, little brother mine, and I heard my name called. I started up. A voice was whispering at my very ear. 'Look out to-morrow!' it said, 'I am coming.' And so it befell twice. Now look! wouldst thou believe it? the idea stuck to me—I scold myself for my folly, and yet I look for Him, our little Father Christ!"

Stepanuich shook his head and said nothing, but he drank his cup dry and put it aside. Then Avdyeeich took up the cup and filled it again.

"Drink some more. 'Twill do thee good. Now it seems to me that when our little Father went about on earth, He despised no one, but sought unto the simple folk most of all. He was always among the simple folk. Those disciples of His too, He chose most of them from amongst our brother-laborers, sinners like unto us. He that exalteth himself, He says, shall be abased, and he that abaseth himself shall be exalted. Ye, says He, call me Lord, and I, says He, wash your feet. He who would be the first among you, He says, let him become the servant of all. And therefore it is that He says, Blessed are the lowly, the peacemakers, the humble, and the long-suffering."

Stepanuich forgot his tea. He was an old man, soft-hearted, and tearful. He sat and listened, and the tears rolled down his cheeks.

"Come, drink a little more," said Avdyeeich. But Stepanuich crossed himself, expressed his thanks, pushed away his cup, and got up.

"I thank thee, Martin Avdyeeich. I have fared well at thy hands, and thou hast refreshed me both in body and soul."

"Thou wilt show me a kindness by coming again. I am so glad to have a guest," said Avdyeeich. Stepanuich departed, and Martin poured out the last drop of tea, drank it, washed up, and again sat down by the window to work—he had some back-stitching to do. He stitched and stitched, and now and then cast glances at the window—he was looking for Christ, and could think of nothing but Him and His works. And the divers sayings of Christ were in his head all the time.

Two soldiers passed by, one in regimental boots, the other in boots of his own making; after that, the owner of the next house passed by in nicely brushed goloshes. A baker with a basket also passed by. All these passed by in turn, and then there came alongside the window a woman in worsted stockings and rustic shoes, and as she was passing by she stopped short in front of the partition wall. Avdyeeich looked up at her from his window, and he saw that the woman was a stranger and poorly clad, and that she had a little child with her. She was leaning up against the wall with her back to the wind, and tried to wrap the child up, but she had nothing to wrap it up with. The woman wore summer clothes, and thin enough they were. And from out of his corner Avdyeeich heard the child crying and the woman trying to comfort it, but she could not. Then Avdyeeich got up, went out of the door and on to the steps, and cried, "My good woman! My good woman!"

The woman heard him and turned round. "Why dost thou stand out in the cold there with the child? Come inside! In the warm room thou wilt be better able to tend him. This way!"

The woman was amazed. What she saw was an old fellow in an apron and with glasses on his nose calling to her. She came towards him. They went down the steps together—they went into the room. The old man led the woman to the bed. "There," said he, "sit down, gossip, nearer to the stove, and warm and feed thy little one...."

He went to the table, got some bread and a dish, opened the oven door, put some cabbage soup into the dish, took out a pot of gruel, but it was not quite ready, so he put some cabbage soup only into the dish, and placed it on the table. Then he fetched bread, took down the cloth from the hook, and spread it on the table.

"Sit down and have something to eat, gossip," said he, "and I will sit down a little with the youngster. I have had children of my own, and know how to manage them." The woman crossed herself, sat down at the table, and began to eat, and Avdyeeich sat down on the bed with the child. Avdyeeich smacked his lips at him again and again, but his lack of teeth made it a clumsy joke at best. And all the time the child never left off shrieking. Then Avdyeeich hit upon the idea of shaking his finger at him, so he snapped his fingers up and down, backwards and forwards, right in front of the child's mouth. He did not put his finger into its mouth, because his finger was black and sticky with cobbler's wax. And the child stared at the finger and was silent, and presently it began to laugh. And Avdyeeich was delighted. But the woman went on eating, and told him who she was and whence she came.

"I am a soldier's wife," she said: "my eight months' husband they drove right away from me, and nothing has been heard of him since. I took a cook's place till I became a mother. They could not keep me *and* the child. It is now three months since I have been drifting about without any fixed resting-place. I have eaten away my all. I wanted to be a wet-nurse, but people wouldn't have me: 'Thou art too thin,' they said. I have just been to the merchant's wife where our grandmother lives, and there they promised to take me in. I thought it was all right, but she told me to come again in a week. But she lives a long way off. I am chilled to death, and he is quite tired out. But God be praised! our landlady has compassion on us, and gives us shelter for Christ's sake. But for that I don't know how we could live through it all."

Avdyeeich sighed, and said, "And have you no warm clothes?"

"Ah, kind friend! this is indeed warm-clothes time, but yesterday I pawned away my last shawl for two *grivenki*."

The woman went to the bed and took up the child, but Avdyeeich stood up, went to the wall cupboard, rummaged about a bit, and then brought back with him an old jacket.

"Look!" said he, "'tis a shabby thing, 'tis true, but it will do to wrap up in."

The woman looked at the old jacket, then she gazed at the old man, and, taking the jacket, fell a-weeping. Avdyeeich also turned away, crept under the bed, drew out a trunk and seemed to be very busy about it, whereupon he again sat down opposite the woman.

Then the woman said: "Christ requite thee, dear little father! It is plain that it was He who sent me by thy window. When I first came out it was warm, and now it has turned very cold. And He it was, little father, who made thee look out of the window and have compassion on wretched me."

Avdyeeich smiled slightly, and said: "Yes, He must have done it, for I looked not out of the window in vain, dear gossip!"

And Avdyeeich told his dream to the soldier's wife also, and how he had heard a voice promising that the Lord should come to him that day.

"All things are possible," said the woman. Then she rose up, put on the jacket, wrapped it round her little one, and then began to curtsey and thank Avdyeeich once more.

"Take this for Christ's sake," said Avdyeeich, giving her a two-grivenka piece, "and redeem your shawl." The woman crossed herself, Avdyeeich crossed himself, and then he led the woman to the door.

The woman went away. Avdyeeich ate up the remainder of the cabbage soup, washed up, and again sat down to work. He worked on and on, but he did not forget the window, and whenever the window was darkened he immediately looked up to see who was passing. Acquaintances passed, strangers passed, but there was no one in particular.

But now Avdyeeich sees how, right in front of his window, an old woman, a huckster, has taken her stand. She carries a basket of apples. Not many now remained; she had evidently sold them nearly all. Across her shoulder she carried a sack full of shavings. She must have picked them up near some new building, and was taking them home with her. It was plain that the sack was straining her shoulder. She wanted to shift it on to the other shoulder, so she rested the sack on the pavement, placed the apple-basket on a small post, and set about shaking down the shavings in the sack. Now while she was shaking down the sack, an urchin in a ragged cap suddenly turned up, goodness knows from whence, grabbed at one of the apples in the basket, and would have made off with it, but the wary old woman turned quickly round and gripped the youth by the sleeve. The lad fought and tried to tear himself loose, but the old woman seized him with both hands, knocked his hat off, and tugged hard at his hair. The lad howled, and the old woman reviled him. Avdyeeich did not stop to put away his awl, but pitched it on the floor, rushed into the courtyard, and in his haste stumbled on the steps and dropped his glasses. Avdyeeich ran out into the street. The old woman was tugging at the lad's hair and wanted to drag him off to the police, while the boy fought and kicked.

"I didn't take it," said he. "What are you whacking me for? Let me go!"

Avdyeeich came up and tried to part them. He seized the lad by the arm and said: "Let him go, little mother! Forgive him for Christ's sake!"

"I'll forgive him so that he shan't forget the taste of fresh birch-rods. I mean to take the rascal to the police station." Avdyeeich began to entreat with the old woman.

"Let him go, little mother; he will not do so any more. Let him go for Christ's sake."

The old woman let him go. The lad would have bolted, but Avdyeeich held him fast.

"Beg the little mother's pardon," said he, "and don't do such things any more. I saw thee take them."

Then the lad began to cry and beg pardon.

"Well, that's all right! And now, there's an apple for thee." And Avdyeeich took one out of the basket and gave it to the boy. "I'll pay thee for it, little mother," he said to the old woman.

"Thou wilt ruin them that way, the blackguards," said the old woman. "If I had the rewarding of him, he should not be able to sit down for a week."

"Oh, little mother, little mother!" cried Avdyeeich, "that is our way of looking at things, but it is not God's way. If we ought to be whipped so for the sake of one apple, what do we deserve for our sins!"

The old woman was silent.

And Avdyeeich told the old woman about the parable of the master who forgave his servant a very great debt, and how that servant immediately went out and caught his fellow-servant by the throat because he was his debtor. The old woman listened to the end, and the lad listened too.

"God bade us forgive," said Avdyeeich, "otherwise He will not forgive us. We must forgive every one, especially the thoughtless."

The old woman shook her head and sighed.

"That's all very well," she said, "but they are spoiled enough already."

"Then it is for us old people to teach them better," said Avdyeeich.

"So say I," replied the old woman. "I had seven of them at one time, and now I have but a single daughter left." And the old woman began telling him where and how she lived with her daughter, and how many grandchildren she had. "I'm not what I was," she said, "but I work all I can. I am sorry for my grandchildren, and good children they are, too. No one is so glad to see me as they are. Little Aksyutka will go to none but me. 'Grandma dear! darling grandma!'" and the old woman was melted to tears. "As for him," she added, pointing to the lad, "boys will be boys, I suppose. Well, God be with him!"

Now just as the old woman was about to hoist the sack on to her shoulder, the lad rushed forward and said:

"Give it here, and I'll carry it for thee, granny! It is all in my way."

The old woman shook her head, but she did put the sack on the lad's shoulder.

And so they trudged down the street together side by side. And the old woman forgot to ask Avdyeeich for the money for the apple. Avdyeeich kept standing and looking after them, and heard how they talked to each other, as they went, about all sorts of things. Avdyeeich followed them with his eyes till they were out of sight, then he turned homewards and found his glasses on the steps (they were not broken), picked up his awl, and sat down to work again. He worked away for a little while, but soon he was scarcely able to distinguish the stitches, and he saw the lamplighter going round to light the lamps. "I see it is time to light up," thought he, so he trimmed his little lamp, lighted it, and again sat down to work. He finished one boot completely, turned it round and inspected it. "Good!" he cried. He put away his tools, swept up the cuttings, removed the brushes and tips, put away the awl, took down the lamp, placed it on the table, and took down the Gospels from the shelf. He wanted to find the passage where he had last evening placed a strip of morocco leather by way of a marker, but he lit upon another place. And just as Avdyeeich opened the Gospel, he recollected his dream of yesterday evening. And no sooner did he call it to mind than it seemed to him as if some persons were moving about and shuffling with their feet behind him. Avdyeeich glanced round and saw that somebody was indeed standing in the dark corner—yes, some one was really there, but who, he could not exactly make out. Then a voice whispered in his ear:

"Martin! Martin! dost thou not know me?"

"Who art thou!" cried Avdyeeich.

"'Tis I," cried the voice, "lo, 'tis I!" And forth from the dark corner stepped Stepanuich. He smiled, and it was as though a little cloud were breaking, and he was gone.

"It is I!" cried the voice, and forth from the corner stepped a woman with a little child; and the woman smiled and the child laughed, and they also disappeared.

"And it is I!" cried the voice, and the old woman and the lad with the apple stepped forth, and both of them smiled, and they also disappeared.

And the heart of Avdyeeich was glad. He crossed himself, put on his glasses, and began to read the Gospels at the place where he had opened them. And at the top of the page He read these words: "And I was an hungered and thirsty, and ye gave Me to drink. I was a stranger and ye took Me in."

And at the bottom of the page he read this: "Inasmuch as ye have done it to the least of these My brethren, ye have done it unto Me."

And Avdyeeich understood that his dream had not deceived him, and that the
Saviour had really come to him that day, and he had really received Him.

The End